THE CHALLENGE
OF CROSS-CULTURAL COMPETENCY
IN SOCIAL WORK

THE CHALLENGE
OF CROSS-CULTURAL COMPETENCY
IN SOCIAL WORK

Experiences of Southeast Asian Refugees
in the United States

Jean Schuldberg

Mellen Studies in Social Work
Volume 7

The Edwin Mellen Press
Lewiston•Queenston•Lampeter

Library of Congress Cataloging-in-Publication Data

Schuldberg, Jean.
   The challenge of cross-cultural competency in social work : experiences of Southeast
Asian refugees in the United States / Jean Schuldberg.
      p. cm. -- (Mellen studies in social work ; v. 7)
   Includes bibliographical references and index.
   ISBN 0-7734-6086-1
   1. Social work with minorities--United States. 2. Social work with immigrants--United
States. 3. Cross-cultural counseling--United States. 4. Intercultural communication--United
States. 5. Refugees--Services for--United States. 6. Yao (Southeast Asian
people)--Services for--United States. 7. Yao Americans (Asian Americans)--Services for.
8. Social work education--United States. I. Title. II. Series.

HV3186.A2S34 2005
362.84'00973

                                                                          2005047850

This is volume 7 in the continuing series
Mellen Studies in Social Work
Volume 7 ISBN 0-7734-6086-1
MSSW Series ISBN 0-7734-7353-X

A CIP catalog record for this book is available from the British Library

The Edwin Mellen Press
Box 450
Lewiston, New York
USA 14092-0450

The Edwin Mellen Press
Box 67
Queenston, Ontario
CANADA L0S 1L0

The Edwin Mellen Press, Ltd.
Lampeter, Ceredigion, Wales
UNITED KINGDOM SA48 8LT

Printed in the United States of America

For Tom

Table of Contents

List of Tables

Table

Preface

Cultural Competency and a New Immigrant Group

By Tony Waters

Over 10,000 Iu-Mien refugees from Laos made their way from remote mountains of Southeast Asia to the United States in the 1980s and 1990s. They were new to the modern United States, and as with all immigrants they were confronted with the dilemma of how to adapt to a new society, while preserving a sense of their own identity. As *The Challenge of Cross-Cultural Competency in Social Work: Experiences of Southeast Asian Refugees in the United States* describes, the social work profession is at the forefront in negotiating the dilemma of acculturation in the context of cultural preservation.

Well aware of the dilemma of integrating people from lands and cultures very different from the middle-class American culture, the social work profession has long required potential social workers to take classes in "cultural competency." The purposes of these requirements are to insure that future social workers are aware of cultures they might work with. The courses are typically fact-oriented surveys of well-established ethnic groups, particularly African-Americans. Emphasized in the courses are the explicit and obvious "low context" differences between the dominant Euro-American middle class culture and the societies future social workers are likely to interact with. Thus, the histories, types of food, language, slang, dress, music, and other explicit differences are emphasized. But, how did such competency training prepare social workers to deal refugees like the Iu-Mien, who arrived from rural Laos in California in the 1980s? How well did cultural competency classes prepare social workers to deal with a small society in which unwritten and even unspoken "high context" understandings about the nature of consensus, conflict, saving face, and respect of elders play a major role? Jean Schuldberg answers this question in an innovative fashion: she asks eight Iu-Mien social service workers—that is people who have been exposed to the cultural competency training themselves—what their experience was with the American social workers they encountered upon arrival.

What Schuldberg finds is that despite formal certification programs in "cross-cultural competency," the provision of social services to new groups like the Iu-Mien is still highly dependent on *ad hoc* adaptation without reference to formal competency training. This is particularly the case with a small and new group like the Iu-Mien, which is unlikely to deal with the general cultural competency courses in a social work program. She writes that the consequence is that well-meaning social workers aware of only the "what" of cross-cultural competency fail to see the "process" needed to integrate effectively into an immigrant society like that of the Iu Mien.

Schuldberg's book really though tells *two* unusual stories. The first is a fairly straightforward account of how a small group of people from Laos, the Iu-Mien, arrived in California. In this respect it is a story of the Iu-Mien that may be told in a standard cultural competency course, such as that she evaluates. But there is a second story, too, which is about why immigration is a process, and how cultural competency training can more effectively prepare social workers to recognize this process. This second story is told through the words of the Iu-Mien social service workers interviewed. Their words ultimately challenge the relevance of the "low context" histories offered in traditional cultural competency training.

The First Story: Misunderstandings in Southeast Asia, Misunderstandings
in the United States

As with other small Southeast Asian ethnic groups, the Iu-Mien created a military to support the American sponsored governments in Laos during the 1960s and 1970s. The first part of the book is a straightforward history describing how an agrarian people living in the remote hills of Laos became embroiled in

America's Indochina wars. Like the Hmong in Laos, and the Montagnards in Vietnam, the Iu-Mien fielded an army, suffered extraordinary casualties, and, after the fall of the American-supported government of Laos, fled to refugee camps in Thailand. It was in Thailand in the 1970s and 1980s that the Iu-Mien people first began to deal with the social service professions who prepared them for resettlement in the United States. Parts of this story have been told before, but the advantage of Schuldberg's account here is that an emphasis is placed on how programs in Thailand prepared—and did not prepare—Iu Mien refugees for life in the United States

In Thai refugee camps of the 1970s-1990s, the United States Department of State funded programs to train refugees in the "realities" of American social life. Beginning as simply English lessons, the programs eventually came to include what designers called a "life skills" oriented approach, focused on use of telephone, banking procedures, job-seeking strategies, and other skills which Schuldberg notes might more precisely be called "idealized version of middle class, Euro-American culture." Not surprisingly, these programs were viewed as successes by the implementing agencies. But, as Schuldberg points out later in the book, what they missed was the fact that such programs, while perhaps well-designed by Euro-American standards, undermined Iu-Mien cultural values of consensus, deference, saving face, and respect for the authority of elders which were the basis for inter-generational stability. In particular this happened as younger people, who had a better command of English than their elders, were deferred to by social service workers focused on getting "the message" across, in whatever manner possible.

The next experience with social service workers for the Iu-Mien came in the United States where they settled in apartment complexes of California's Central Valley. Social workers accustomed to assertive clients, expected Iu-Mien refugees would be aggressive in their requests for service. In short, they assumed the type of explicit "low context" communication of people who "know the rules" meaning clients who had experience with in Euro-American culture, or for that matter, African-American culture. Instead, often unnoticed by the social workers, was a Iu-Mien society which valued highly consensus and family authority, more than the explicit written rules. The Iu-Mien often communicated this quietly, but only through deferential "high context" communication whether dealing with their own elders, or the high status social workers with whom they came in contact. Instead of recognizing the quiet deference for what it was, middle-class social workers interpreted "the silences" of refugees who would not contradict elders or for that matter the high status social workers, as agreement and acquiescence.

A good example of the miscommunication is indicated with references to a memory related by one of the Iu-Mien social service workers interviewed, who recalls a social worker telling her "You are lying to me, there was no such war." Apparently because the American social worker had never heard about the Iu-Mien, or that they fought with the United States in Laos, whether in a cultural competency class or elsewhere, she assumed the war had never occurred. In a low context society like the middle class United States the absence of such a legitimated source apparently implied that the events described were impossible. Without an explicit assertion from a text, classroom lecture, expert, cultural competency course, or classroom lecture, the social worker apparently felt that her own competency was challenged; the only retort was the pithy assertion of the title.

The Second Story: Views of the Iu-Mien Social Workers

Schuldberg's response to the social work profession is about the nature of cultural competency training. This response comes from in-depth interviews with her respondents who are all Iu-Mien refugees themselves, as well as being employees of social service agencies where they have regular contact with social workers. Included were initial interviews, follow-up interviews, and on-going collaboration with interviewees to probe the deeper context of interaction between the social service professions, and Iu-Mien refugees. Skillfully using such interview techniques Schuldberg identifies a pattern in how conventional social service practices, designed by a mainstream culture which values low context bluntness and explicit instruction, is inadequate for dealing with a society for whom saving face, deference, and consensus are more important. Repeatedly, the refrain from the Iu-Mien social service workers was that in the context of a new culture, the social worker should simply "ask" in a polite way. Misunderstanding, they emphasized, was not because a social worker did not know an explicit fact about the culture, but because social workers did not ask "why?" questions, and instead jumped to conclusions and interpretations rooted in understandings drawn from the dominant middle class culture. In essence, the flawed assumption was that since the Iu-Mien clients did not say something about an arrest, needing medical care, denial of welfare benefits, parent-teacher conferences, etc., they must be in agreement with whatever the social worker asserted.

In urging social workers to ask "why?" questions, the Iu Mien social service workers emphasize that questions that Americans perceive as intrusive may not be so. The emphasis should be on the "process," Schuldberg explains, through which entry to the community is gained. This is more relevant than knowing the low context positivistic facts about history, food, dress, music, religion or culture of a particular group. Common problems, the social service workers recalled included examples ranging from the "coining" treatments used in traditional medicine but occasionally misinterpreted as child abuse, and the over-use of children as interpreters which resulted in the usurpation of parental authority. Failure to observe the importance of the extended family also resulted in stress on family units, which otherwise would have been important coping mechanisms.

Culturally Competent Social Workers and New Immigrants

Schuldberg concludes that a major problem with cultural competency training is not specific knowledge about cultural groups, but developing skills in approaching unfamiliar communities. Cultural competency, she points out, is not only about teaching a survey or the history of a traditionally oppressed group. For social workers, it is also about recognizing that there is a process to how new groups admit outsiders into their confidence in a manner, which makes the provision of social services more effective.

Left unsaid, though is a broader point, which I think is important not just for social work education, but education in general. Training for diversity and "cultural competence" has become a booming business, particularly in a place like California where 25% of the population is foreign-born. But as is implied by Schuldberg's book, immigrants of the future will not be the same as the groups about which facts and histories are being taught to future social workers, teachers, police officers, probation officers, and others who will confront immigrants yet to arrive. The groups, which arrive in the future, will, like the Iu-Mien, be from unexpected places, speak unusual languages, and have unusual customs. Social services of the future will do best by following the advice of Schuldberg's interviewees, and ask, watch, listen, and observe, before jumping to conclusions. They should be trained to recognize and interpret cues from a culture and society very different than their own. The key conclusion of Schuldberg's work is not about the Iu-Mien per se, but that cultural competency itself is ultimately about how to ask, watch, listen and observe.

Tony Waters an Associate Professor and Chair, Department of Sociology, California State University, Chico. He is the author of *Bureaucratizing the Good Samaritan*, (Westview, 2001) and *Crime and Immigrant Youth* (Sage, 1999). He has been writing about issues dealing with refugees from Southeast Asia and elsewhere since 1984.

Acknowledgements

I wish to express my gratitude to the following people for without their support and assistance, this book would not have reached fruition.

I am eternally grateful to my soulmate, Tom Fox, who without his undaunted support, love, and continuous care of our family, I could never have completed the research. I thank my children, Nicky, Louise, and Joey, my mother, Jane Schuldberg, and late father, Irving I. Schuldberg, who supported my dreams. I am also appreciative of my brother, sisters and brother-in-laws, and my mother and father-in-law whose encouragement and love were a guiding force.

I am grateful to my mentor, Dr. Rosita Galang who provided steady support and guidance. Her flexibility and expertise were an inspiration. Father Denis Collins, with his wry humor, led me into a deeper understanding of Paulo Freire. I thank him for his trust and willingness to lend me rare copies of material. Additionally, I am appreciative Dr. Susan Katz whose questions stimulated greater analysis and reflection.

My dear friends and fellow social workers were an integral part of this process. Dr. Pam Johansen was my confidant, counselor, advocate, and more importantly, my friend. Lorie Cavanaugh listed to my incoherent ramblings and soothed my soul. Patty Hunter provided a sense of stability and rationality. Wendy Aviles was a sister in the truest sense. I thank Dr. Celeste Jones for her continuous encouragement and belief in my ability to publish, and careful editing of the manuscript. My colleagues Dr. Evette Castillo, Dr. Debra Luna, Dr. Sharon Willey, and Dr. Lois Moore provided confidence and courage. Dr. Rose Borunda and her students kindly translated from Spanish an obscure chapter written by Paulo Freire.

My colleagues at California State University, Chico provided continual support. Dr. Pamela A. Brown, Professor Jan O'Donnell and Dr. Kathy Kaiser offered encouragement, advice, and faith in my ability to succeed. Dr. Tony Waters generously provided his wisdom and expertise.

I thank Dr. John Rupnow, Director of Edwin Mellen Press and Ms. Patricia Schultz, Production Editor for their support of this text. I also wish to acknowledge Helen E. Thorington for her assistance with the final formatting of the manuscript.

I am most in debt to the individuals who participated in this study: Kim Fahm Chao, Meycho Monica Chao-Lee, Sunny Chinn, Faye Seng Lee, Wernjiem O. Pien, Kao F. Saechao, Koy Saephan, and Chiem-Seng Yaangh. I feel very honored to have been privy to their reflections on their experiences and view of their culture. The participants welcomed me with such grace and warmth and for that I am truly thankful.

Introduction

American, American why am I an alien to you?
Do I not have the same color as you or
is it my eyes that are not blue enough?
Aren't you the one who taught me how to love blond hair and hate my own?

America, America, I though that you were the land of the free
and the land full of Golden Opportunity. . . .
America, why do you hurt me so much
when I am so much a part of you?

(F. L. Saechao, 1999a, pp. 50-51)

The United States is frequently viewed by the general populous as a melting pot, that is, individuals from varying cultures blend together to "share similar national values, behaviors, traditions" (Smith, 2004, p. 333). However, we are actually a nation that is composed of groups maintaining their ethnic identity while adopting aspects of the mainstream (Devore & Schlesinger, 1999). From this perspective, the United States is more culturally pluralistic than a melting pot. That is, we are a nation of multiple cultures that "contribute to the balance, flavor, and beauty of the whole" (Smith, 2004, p. 328).

Social work's history of working with immigrants and refugees continues in the present day, though the immigrants and refugees tend to come from Asia and Central and South American instead of Europe (U.S. Census Bureau, 2001). Because a majority of social workers are EuroAmerican, the need to understand how to enter into cultures other than one's own is critical to successful practice (Morris, 1993). Social work students need training in this area through the undergraduate and graduate curriculum in order to assist clients from the wide ranges of cultures in our society. Students need to gain awareness and respect for those who are different from their home culture, even if that difference is not immediately apparent.

Through my employment in the field of social services, I became aware of the lack of cultural competency that social service staff often exhibited with clients from a range of cultural backgrounds. Similar reports from students at the university level confirmed my concerns. Students' accounts of interactions with colleagues, supervisors, and community leaders who lacked cultural competency led me to research the needs in the field of social work. The primary force for this research resulted from the number of stories from students who were recent refugees from Southeast Asia, particularly those from the Iu-Mien community.

This book is about the need for social work education to address issues of cultural competency from a perspective not documented in the literature. Participatory research was the methodology guiding the focus of this book; therefore, the participants themselves emerge as the central voice of the research. Their stories provide a valuable gift to the field of human services. Their wise, strong, insightful, and optimistic voices will help us combat inequity and oppression. The need for not only acceptance of other cultures, but valuing and appreciating the diversity in the United States is a central theme. As stated in the except in the poem above, as human service workers, we need to work toward combating the inequity and resulting "hurt" for those who are truly a part of us, our national community.

Chapter 1

Cultural Competency:

Social Work In A Culturally Diverse Society

There's a lot of anger that they want to talk about; a lot of anger because there is no recognition. There is no record of what they did. They lost their husbands, their father, their family, and there is no record, "there is no such war."

It used to be that when they come in they talked about why I lost my husband in the Mien war, [social workers would say] "they are too young, what are they talking about? Well, there was a war, but what war? You're lying to me." Staff have actually said to me, "you are lying to me, there was no such war." (Chao-Lee, personal communication, 2001)

The practice of social work in the United States is rooted in work with immigrants and refugees. One branch of social work traditionally focused on helping individuals to assimilate, while the other focused on the celebration of cultural diversity (Trattner, 1974). The need for culturally competent social workers has become a prominent focus of social work education as a result of the increasing diversity in the United States. The 2000 United States Census revealed that 10.4% of Americans were foreign-born and nearly half of all foreign-born were of Latin America origin. Twenty-six percent of those born outside the United States were from Asia. Of the 50 states, California had the largest foreign-born population in 2000, with 26% of the residents born outside the U.S. (U.S. Census Bureau, 2001).

In California alone, the prediction is that the Hispanic population will double and the Asian population will grow by two-thirds from 1990 to 2010. More than half of California's population will be Asian, Hispanic, or African American (LAO, 1996). With over 70% of the Asian population born outside the United States, Hu-DeHart (1999) considers Asians the "fastest growing racial-ethnic population" (p. 7).

Due to the changing demographics, culturally competent social workers are a necessity to meet the various needs of an increasingly diverse population in the United States. The importance of understanding one's own and other peoples' cultures is paramount in the practice of social work (Midgette & Meggert, 1991; Tasker, 1999; Van Voorhis, 1998). Lack of cultural competency may hinder social work practice, that is, the ability to advocate, help broker resources, and support the strengths of individuals and communities. Cultural competency in social work entails awareness of cultural diversity and the ability to work with varying cultural groups in a skillful, sensitive, and knowledgeable fashion (Cross, 1988; Lum, 1999; Raheim, 1995).

As the need for services to address the growing immigrant and refugee population increases, the natural progression is the rise in employment opportunities for social workers. Social work has been described a one of the 20 "hot job tracks," careers that are in demand (Beddingfield, Hawkins, Ito, Lenzy, & Loftus, 1996). Currently, the employment of social workers is expected to increase "faster than average" of all occupations through the year 2006. "Faster than average" means that the employment in a specific field is projected to increase from a growth rate of 21% to a growth rate of 35% between 2002 and 2012 (United States Bureau of Labor Statistics, 2004).

The following qualitative study concentrates on cultural competency in social work practice. The Iu-Mien[1] community was chosen as the population for the study due to their multitude of experiences with social workers through individuals' refugee status. The Iu-Mien community is relatively small when compared to other Southeast Asian refugee groups in the United States. The material available on the community is limited and primarily written by non-Iu-Mien individuals. There is a great need for the voices of the community to be heard by those who serve them.

Social service workers from the Iu-Mien communities in Northern California generously provided rich material on their experiences. The material in the following chapters addresses the Iu-Mien culture, the United States policies and services for Southeast Asian Refugees from the 1970s to the early 1990s, experiences of Iu-Mien individuals with social workers in the United States, and recommendations for teaching cultural competency in social work education. Much of the information this study provides can be generalized to other populations who have experienced oppression and marginalization.

Social Work Education and Cultural Competency: An Overview

The National Association of Social Workers' (NASW) (1997) Code of Ethics views the acquisition of cultural competency as an ethical standard:

---

[1] Gogol (1996) states that Iu-Mien representatives from "several countries" (p. 22) met in 1987 [location not noted in the writing] and decided that Iu-Mien would be the recognized name. This was not mentioned in any of the other literature reviewed for this study. MacDonald (1997) relates that when books are written in the Iu-Mien Unified Script, Iu-Mien is spelled "Iu-Mienh. The "h" indicates tone, "but the /h/ is omitted in general usage among the Iu-Mien in the United States" (MacDonald, 1997, p. xi). The controversy as to the correct spelling continues as Chinn (2000) relates, "when we say Mienh, it is like we say Caucasian or African-American. Mienh is a more polite term. To spell correctly: MIENH. Mien_ with no "H" is unacceptable" (p. 7). For this study, Iu-Mien is the spelling of preference due to the decision made by the representatives in 1987. Additionally, it seems to be the most common usage in the literature that is written by individuals from the Iu-Mien community. The use of Mienh and Mien is used in this text in direct quotes or paraphrases of those citations.

1.05 (a) Social workers should understand culture and its function in human behavior and society, recognizing the strengths that exist in all cultures.

1.05 (b) Social Workers should have a knowledge base of their clients' cultures and be able to demonstrate competence in the provision of services that are sensitive to the clients' cultures and to differences among people and cultural groups.

1.05 (c) Social workers should obtain education about and seek to understand the nature of social diversity and oppression with respect to race, ethnicity, national origin, sex, sexual orientation, age, marital status, political belief, religion and mental or physical disability. (p. 9)

The Council on Social Work Education (CSWE) (1999) mandates the teaching of cultural competency in their guidelines for baccalaureate programs. The 1999 guidelines state that the coursework needs to:

(B5.42) Prepare graduates to practice with diverse populations.

(B5.72) Practice within the values and ethics of the social work profession and with an understanding of and respect for the positive value of diversity.

(B5.74) Understand the forms and mechanisms of oppression and discrimination and the strategies of change that advance social and economic justice. (p. 19)

Additionally, the guidelines state that:

(B6.4) Professional social work education is committed to preparing students to understand and appreciate human diversity. Programs must provide curriculum content about differences and similarities in the experiences, needs and beliefs of people. The curriculum must include content about differential assessment and intervention skills that will enable practitioners to serve diverse populations. Each program is required to include content about population groups that are particularly relevant to the program's mission. These include, but are not limited to, groups distinguished by race, ethnicity, culture, class, gender, sexual orientation, religion, physical or mental disability, age, and national origin. (p. 21)

The social work literature described many different methods for providing students the opportunity to learn about diverse cultures including cultural immersion and student inter-group dialogues (Nagda, Spearmon, Holley, Harding, Balassone, Moise-Swanson, & de Mello, 1999; Poole, 1998). Current literature tends to focus on assessing the effectiveness of teaching cultural competency in social work education, on social workers' perceptions of cultural competency, and social workers' experiences in the field with applying their knowledge in this area.

Students are eager to learn of other cultures if the experiences can be situated in their everyday lives. However, most texts and class formats tend to reproduce stereotypes in the attempt to educate for cultural sensitivity and, in turn, cultural competency. Social work education has presented an Eurocentric focus in the development of curriculum (Castex, 1993; Graham, 1999; Mason, Benjamin, & Lewis, 1996; McMahon & Allen-Meares, 1992).

Members of non-dominant groups in the United States who have received services from social workers are not represented in the current literature that assesses social work needs in the teaching of cultural competency. I have not found research that specifically addresses the perspective from members of non-dominant groups in the United States in regard to their experiences with social workers who were culturally competent and/or social workers who demonstrated lack of cultural competency.

Iu-Mien Social Workers as Participants

The Iu-Mien people in the United States represent a relatively small minority group of refugees from Southeast Asia. Through refugee resettlement and entitlement programs, most Iu-Mien adults have experienced contact with social workers upon entrance in the United States in such settings as refugee assistance, federal and state family support programs, adult and child protective services, medical providers, schools, and correctional institutions. Social service workers from the Iu-Mien community have the unique position of having received services and now providing them. Thus, they have experienced contact with non-Iu-Mien social service workers in various roles and settings.

8

The Iu-Mien people have a unique history with the United States government that led to their immigration to this country. The majority of the Iu-Mien population in the United States was refugees from Laos who were recruited by the United States Central Intelligence Agency (CIA) to prevent North Vietnamese troops from bringing supplies through the region en route to South Vietnam. This occurred from 1960-1975 and was termed by the United States, and later the Iu-Mien and Hmong (another highland group), as "The Secret War of the CIA" (Habbard, 1987; Smith & Tarallo, 1993). The Iu-Mien journey from Laos to refugee camps in Thailand was difficult and many were killed or died during their journey to the camps.

In 1978, the first groups of Iu-Mien refugees arrived in the United States. The literature has indicated that Southeast Asian refugees, including the Iu-Mien people, have experienced great difficulty in adapting to the American way of life (Chao, 1999; Smith & Tarallo, 1993). This is due to the extreme contrast between the Iu-Mien's rural lifestyle in Laos and contemporary Euro-American culture (Chao, 1999; Habarad, 1987a; Pon, 1984; Strouse, 1989).

In the world today, the Iu-Mien population is considered small, that is, less than 1.5 million (Houghton, 1989) or approximately 2,672,110 (MacDonald, 1997) depending on the source. There are approximately 32,000 Iu-Mien in the United States, with 27, 920 residing in California (MacDonald, 1997). A large percentage of the Iu-Mien people have chosen to settle in Northern California, including 9,500 in Sacramento, 2,500 in Redding, and 1,000 in Oroville (MacDonald, 1997).

Purpose of the Study

This research describes the experiences of Iu-Mien social service workers with non-Iu-Mien social workers when they were clients and currently as workers. Specifically, it is to:

a. Describe Iu-Mien social service workers' experiences with non-Iu-Mien social workers that were perceived by the Iu-Mien social service workers as displaying cultural competency or lacking in cultural competency.

b. Generate recommendations for content areas for inclusion in courses teaching cultural competency in undergraduate social work education.

Research Questions

The following questions are addressed in this research:

1. As previous recipients of social services, what have been Iu-Mien social service workers' experiences with non-Iu-Mien social workers in the United States?

2. As practitioners, what were the Iu-Mien social service workers' experiences with non-Iu-Mien social workers?

3. In what ways did Iu-Mien social service workers feel non-Iu-Mien social workers were culturally competent?

4. In what ways did Iu-Mien social service workers feel non-Iu-Mien social workers demonstrated lack of cultural competency?

5. What themes emerged from the Iu-Mien social service workers' experiences with non-Iu-Mien social workers that indicated areas to be included in courses teaching cultural competency in undergraduate social work education?

Theoretical Framework

The theoretical framework for this study is derived from the following: (a) Freirian view of social workers as "extension agents," and (b) sociological theories of ethnocentrism, assimilation, and cultural pluralism that relate to social work education and practice.

Freirian View of Social Workers as "Extension Agents"

Paulo Freire's (1985) discussion of social workers as extension agents provided this study with a rich theoretical base. Freire's work is important because it frames social work, and social work education, as a political act.

10

During the research process, I worked *with* the Iu-Mien social service workers to listen to, and reflect on their experiences. The social service workers' reflections of non-Iu-Mien social workers' roles as "extension agents" guide my recommendations for changing the content and process of training within the educational system. Thus, an outcome goal of the dialectic process and development of generative themes is an action, a praxis, to change the social structure. That is, recommendations for changes in the teaching of cultural competency for the Council on Social Work Education, the National Association of Social Workers, and the educational community.

Freire (1985) analyzed social workers in regard to their role as instruments of oppression. Additionally, he evaluated social workers' relationships with clients in the role as collaborative agents of change (Freire, 1999). Freire's analysis complements the assessment of social work education from a sociological perspective.

Sociological Theories: Application in Social Work

Social work has a long history of focusing on caring for those in need beginning in the United States during the 1600s. Over time, the field expanded to include the development of programs for prevention and assistance with social problems and a focus on advocating for social change (Trattner, 1974). Ethnocentrism and the ideology of assimilation have impacted the development of the field of social work and social work education. Ethnocentrism is the "tendency to believe that the norms and values of one's own culture are superior to those of others, and to use these norms as a standard when evaluating all other cultures" (Bryjak & Soroka, 1997, p. 531). For the social work profession, Graham (1999) related that an " . . . ethnocentric knowledge base places limitations on the development of social work and calls into question the integrity and legitimacy of the profession" (p. 104).

Assimilation is defined as the "process in which minority groups become absorbed or incorporated into the majority group's sociocultural system" (Bryjak

& Soroka, 1997, p. 529). Potocky (1997) discussed a trend in the United States that calls for "a return to assimilation ideology" and stated that from a social work perspective, the profession has "an obligation to take action against such racist and assimilationist attitudes and behaviors" (p. 319).

In this light, the emphasis on cultural pluralism, a multicultural approach that acknowledges the oppression in our society, has increasingly become a theme of social work education. Cultural pluralism provides the " . . . premise that U.S. society should not be characterized as having only one national culture, but rather it should be seen as having a national culture as well as many distinct cultural groups" (Fellin, 2000, p. 262).

Scope and Delimitation of the Study

The participants in the study were adults, aged 18 years and older, from the Iu-Mien community who were currently employed in social service settings in the role of a social service worker. The study focused on their perceptions of interactions with non-Iu-Mien social service workers and/or social workers, evaluating areas where the workers demonstrated cultural competency and/or seemed to lack cultural competency. The data obtained from this study have been used to make recommendations for specific course content in undergraduate social work programs.

Limitations of the Study

There are several possible limitations of the study. The participants in this study may not be representative of the Iu-Mien adult social service workers' population. This is because the participants were not chosen by random sampling, therefore, the information may not be generalizable to the general population of Iu-Mien social service workers. Due to the qualitative nature of the study, it consisted of a small sample of eight individuals who were invited to share their experiences. The small sample enabled me to conduct a comprehensive study of the critical reflections of the participants. Although the sample was limited, the participants provided in-depth insight into their personal experiences with non-Iu-Mien social workers.

The dialogues occurred in the participants' places of employment, restaurants, their homes, and university centers, per request of each of the participants. It is important to note that the natural setting of the home might have inhibited some sharing of information when other family members were present. Of other concern, the work setting might have inhibited information sharing due to its formal ambience and possible concerns that co-workers or supervisors might not be supportive of the topic. Another important factor in this study was that I am EuroAmerican and do not speak Iu-Mien, Lao, Thai, or Chinese. Cultural difference might have affected the type of data that were collected.

The NASW Code of Ethics (1997) provides guidance to social workers in regard to behaviors toward colleagues such as respect, and indicates ways to address incompetence or unethical behavior. Additionally, the Code relates that social workers need to maintain the integrity of the profession by voicing issues of oppression and working with the greater society for social justice and equity. However, it is important to note also the unspoken rule or "code of etiquette" in social work that a social service worker or social worker does not speak negatively of a colleague out of professional respect. This proscriptive norm can conflict with the Social Work Code of Ethics. Thus, etiquette may have impacted the type of information that was shared with me. The design of participatory research with multiple occasions for dialogue did help to build relationships with the participants that fostered open, honest communication.

Significance of the Study

The findings of this study provide information on non-Iu-Mien social workers' interactions with the Iu-Mien, members of a non-dominant group in the United States. Thus, highlighting the unique perspective of a former client who was now in a role as the social service worker. This research offers new ways of approaching the issue of teaching cultural competency in undergraduate social work education. The review of the literature indicates a need for studies that focus on the experiences of recipients of social services and the experiences of social service workers from non-dominant groups with their social work colleagues. The dialogues provide insights into the impact of cultural misunderstanding that were a result of negligent cultural competency.

The methods through which cultural competency is presented vary greatly from school to school. Some universities provide a semester-long course that is entirely focused on students' gaining self-awareness of their own culture and value systems while integrating information about the diverse cultures within the United States. Other programs integrate the teaching of cultural diversity in all of the required social work courses including social policy, research, and practice. Thus, the content and the teaching model may be dependent on the structure of the program and the individual who teaches the course.

The value base of social work and the mandates by the Council on Social Work Education demonstrate the need for the development of a comprehensive curriculum for social work undergraduate students. There seems to be little guidance in regard to the content and methods of teaching cultural competency from either the National Association of Social Workers or the Council on Social Work Education.

For the educator, the information from this research has the potential to increase her or his understanding of the impact of social workers. Understanding the Iu-Mien's individual experiences with social workers provides insight into the cultural competency need in social work education. The experiences of the participants will help to broader knowledge of what it means to be cultural competent. With the rapidly changing demographics of our nation and the increased need for social workers, the development of cultural competency in social workers is seen not only as a value within the profession, but a necessity.

Chapter 2

A Historical Background of Southeast Asian Refugees

The historical background of the Southeast Asian refugees is paramount in understanding issues of cultural competency. The following discussion includes two parts: (a) the Southeast Asian refugee experience prior to immigrating to the United States, and (b) the Southeast Asian refugee experience in California. Since the Iu-Mien population is quite small in comparison to other Southeast Asian groups, the literature on the refugee experience tends to provide a general view of the experiences of all groups including those from the Iu-Mien, Hmong, Vietnamese, and Cambodian populations. Thus, this chapter includes some information about the other groups.

The Southeast Asian Refugee Experience Prior to Immigrating
to the United States
Definition of a Refugee

The United States Department of the State defines a refugee as:

> . . . a person who has fled his or her country of origin because of a well-founded fear of persecution based on race, religion, nationality, political opinion or membership in a particular social group. This definition of a "refugee" excludes people who have left their homes only to seek a more prosperous life. Such people are commonly called 'economic immigrants,' and are not refugees. People fleeing civil wars and natural disasters also may not be eligible for refugee resettlement under U. S. law,

> though they may come under the protection of the United Nations High Commissioner for Refugees (UNHCR). (U.S. Dept of State, 2000, p. 1)

In order to qualify as a refugee, individuals in Southeast Asian refugee camps were interviewed by an officer from the U.S. Immigration and Naturalization Service (INS). The officer decided if the individual was considered a refugee by the United States guidelines. Therefore, it was important for a person to leave their country of origin and enter a refugee camp in another country to demonstrate that they were leaving due to fear of persecution. As stated by the U.S. State Department, "the preferred solution for most refugees is to return home as soon as it is safe for them to do so" (U.S. Dept. of State, 2000, p.1). Repatriation is reported as a fear for many to this day who remain in refugee camps due to stories of "people being forced back to Laos where they are little more than slaves or where they may be killed" (Lindsay, 1996, p. 2). For over 2,000 Iu-Mien in 1994, repatriation to Laos was a reality (Saetern, 2000).

Most of the world's refugees are not from Western countries. Indra (1999) related, in regard to refugees that

> Most of the world's forced migrants are neither Northern natives nor are they located in Northern countries. But academics, other researchers, government policymakers, and international agencies from the North dominate much discussion and action involving forced migrants, and hence chiefly frame relevant institutions, agencies, programs, and communities in virtually every part of the world. (p. 3)

Thus, I feel that it is important to critically read the literature that is written about refugees and public policy to evaluate the origin and source of the writings. Indra (1999) further stated that

> A majority of the world's forced migrants are at least temporarily unable to control key dimensions of their existence . . . Whether they wish it or not, they and forced migrants often are unequally located in structures of interpretation, representation, decision-making, policy generation, and program delivery. (p. 19)

Refugee Camps and Processing Centers
United States Legislation Affecting Refugees Overseas

The United States has a history of opening its doors to immigrants and refugees. However, the doors have opened in varying degrees depending on the country of origin, economic situation in the United States, and the political orientation of the group seeking entrance. Quotas and restrictions have been placed on many groups, the most widely known being the Chinese in the 1880s. The Immigration and Nationality Act of 1965 (P.L. 89-236) focused on family reunification and the immigration of those with transferable skills that were needed in the United States. Quotas that were determined by national origin were discontinued with this Act.

When the "first wave" of Southeast Asian refugees began to arrive in the United States in 1975, the "response to the refugee flows reflected humanitarian and foreign policy concerns . . . [the] refugee situation [was seen] as symbolic of the problems of living under communism" (McBride, 1999, p. 10). The political culture of the time was anti-Communist. Thus, the doors to the United States were opened wide to those who were seen as victims of Communist oppression.

Due to the increase in the numbers of Southeast Asian refugees in the late 1970s, The Refugee Act of 1980 (P.L. 96-212) was implemented by the Department of State and the Department of Justice. The Department of State funded the Joint Voluntary Agency to coordinate the programming. The State Department funded the United Nations High Commissioner for Refugees (UNHCR) to operate the camps within the Thai Ministry of Interior. The Department of State chose organizations that were private, nongovernmental, to facilitate English as a Second Language (ESL) and later, Cultural Orientation (CO) and Work Orientation (WO) classes in the camps and processing centers in Phanat Nikhom, Thailand and Bataan, the Philippines.

The beginning camps for Southeast Asian refugees were described as "primitive . . . [due to a] concern that to provide more than basic services was to risk attracting more refugees" (Harmon, 1995, p. 25). However, by 1984, the camps were described as a "full-fledged community that included open-air markets, temples and churches, hospitals . . . outdoor cafes" (Ranard & Pfleger, 1995, p. 39). Saetern (1998) noted that residents in the refugee camps were not allowed to raise livestock or farm because foods such as cabbage and rice were to be provided by the United Nations. She stated, "living in the camp was very harsh under the Thai authority and people did not have any freedom" (p. 31).

Some refugee camps were described by residents as dangerous places that required children to be watchful guards for their families. Rapes reportedly were not uncommon (Lemberger, 1996). Giles (1999) related that refugee camps could be viewed as "both places of refuge from the nationalist and gendered violence of war, as well as sites of gendered violence" (p. 90). This seemed true in regard to stories from Southeast Asian refugees.

Refugee camps were also described by residents as places of despair and crisis. One young refugee reported:

> The living conditions of the camp were really bad. There was dust flying all around and in the rainy season the rains would create a lot of flooded . . . . every camp there was a fence to keep us in and the outside out . . . [it] was barbed wire . . . . (Moua, 2000, ¶ 5)

His view was substantiated by Chinn's (2000) vivid presentation:

> There were 25,000 refugees living in a twenty acres of land surrounded by armed and no mercy solders. Diseases and bacteria were beyond control. Trash and human waste were everywhere. No communication was allowed from the refugee to outsiders. It was terrible to live there. One day is like one year. (p. 2)

The literature describing the programs that were implemented in the camps does not address the violence reported by refugees or specific descriptions of the living conditions.

Refugees initially lived in "first asylum camps" on the border, the camps of first origin. Once she or he was determined eligible for refugee status, the refugee was moved to a "processing center transit camp" while awaiting admission to the country of resettlement (Harmon, 1995). For the Iu-Mien people, this meant that processing centers were located in Phanat Nikhom, Thailand and in Bataan, Philippines. The camps in Galang, Indonesia primarily served the Vietnamese. These processing sites were operated by different groups and will be discussed individually later in this book. All sites provided programs to prepare the refugee, at a minimal level during the early years of the camps' existence, for immigration to the host country.

Profile of the Teachers

Ranard and Pfleger (1995) reported that the teachers in the overseas programs were college graduates who were "highly proficient in English" (p. 60). Refugees were teachers' assistants, and Thai and Filipino nationals became the majority of workers in the program (Ranard & Pfleger, 1995). In some programs, such as the Native Language Literacy program in Thailand, refugees volunteered as teachers; their educational background was varied (Ligon, 1995). Programs also included Thai Primary School, in Thai, for the children.

English as a Second Language (ESL)

The processing centers utilized a curriculum funded through the Overseas Refugee Training Program (ORTP) by the United States Department of State (Liegel, 1991). The Center for Applied Linguistics developed and coordinated this curriculum that focused on English as a Second Language (ESL) for individuals 17-55 years of age. The program was called Competency-Based Adult Education (CBAE) (Liegel, 1991). Participants in the ESL classes were placed in groups depending on their level of native language literacy and proficiency in English.

At first, due to lack of classroom space, the courses at the processing center were limited to one family member who was considered the head of the household (Morgan, 1995; Ranard & Pfleger, 1995). As the years progressed, classroom spaces were enlarged and by 1983, all ages had access to programs. It was during the early 1980s that the awareness of women's roles in the family and the negative impact of isolation in the home became the catalyst for the development of programs for women. Depression was reported in many of the women refugees; courses were then designed to target pregnant women, those with small children, and those who desired home-based employment opportunities (Ranard & Pfleger, 1995).

Specific programs were developed in 1984 for teens to prepare them for the "American high school experience " (Ranard & Pfleger, 1995, p. 52), mimicking the culture that included parent conferences, sports fields, hall passes and report cards, and teenage social and academic language. In 1987, elementary school programs were developed with a focus on linking "language to real experience" (Ranard & Pfleger, 1995, p. 54). By 1993, preschool refugee children attended programs that followed the Head Start model in the United States (Morgan 1995; Ranard & Pfleger, 1995). Programs were developed for those with special needs such as the hearing impaired and those with learning disabilities. Throughout the 1990s, the "final years . . . focused on intergenerational and family issues . . . changing . . . traditional roles" (Morgan, 1995, p. 11).

The topics covered in the ESL class changed over time. Initially, the focus was on basic English, including grammar and general cultural orientation that was needed for introduction into the United States (Harmon, 1995; Ranard & Pfleger, 1995). The subjects in both classes were modified to center more on a lifeskills oriented approach of language acquisition. Topics included the use of a telephone, banking procedures, job-seeking strategies, manners of relating healthcare concerns, and techniques for completing forms. It seems that what was presented in the camps for children and adults was an idealized version of middle class, Euro-American culture. That is to say, it was an extension of the dominant culture.

Innovative approaches were also used to include the participant's life experiences as a medium for the development of literacy skills. Some teachers recorded students' stories, while in other cases, students taped their stories or wrote about films they had viewed (Ranard & Pfleger, 1995). Initially, the programs were traditional with little intergenerational involvement. However, as the years progressed, intergenerational activities were introduced to maintain the culture of community, meet family needs, and decrease the risk for intergenerational conflict (Hoyt, 1995).

Cultural Orientation (CO)

In 1980, the Department of State began a program that "provided refugees with skills needed for resettlement before they enter the United States" (Morgan, 1995, p. 3). This was a direct result of "cultural misunderstandings" (Morgan, 1995, p. 4) that had occurred in the United States. These included incidents of refugees being jailed for not securing hunting licenses, childcare practices that came into conflict with EuroAmerican culture, and injuries from lack of knowledge of the use of household appliances.

The "Cultural Orientation" (CO) program evolved not only from "cultural misunderstandings," but also out of the need to help refugees become better prepared for American lifestyles. Refugees from the rural areas were experiencing "cultural and language shock" when they arrived in the United States as they had "never cooked on a stove, used a telephone, or looked for a job" (Liegel, 1991, p. 44). The CO classes, frequently given in the participant's native language, provided information on social services, health, social graces (such as the use of eye contact which was culturally considered impolite by many participants), and coping strategies for the cultural differences they would encounter (Liegel, 1991; Ranard & Pfleger, 1995).

Work Orientation (WO)

Work Orientation (WO) was added to the overseas refugee program in 1983. It was provided to a participant after she or he had completed 15 weeks of ESL and Cultural Orientation. Work Orientation was taught in English and used vocational ESL (VESL) as a model. The program provided instruction on communication within a work setting and educated about work culture. Many of the refugees' occupational skills were not transferable to the United States, and consequently they needed retraining. Participants were involved in on-the-job training sites for 100 class hours over a 25-day period. The goal of this program was to prepare the refugee for securing employment once resettled and to gain skills for movement beyond entry-level positions (Liegel, 1991).

Processing Center - Phanat Nikhom, Thailand

The processing center in Phanat Nikhom, Thailand, established in 1982, was operated by the Save the Children Federation, Experiment in International Living, and the World Education Program. The center's population consisted of members from the Hmong, Vietnamese, Lahu, Khmer, Lao, and Iu-Mien communities (Ligon, 1995). Ligon (1995) reported that individuals from the Hmong community were interested in first language literacy and as a result, a Native Language Literacy program (NLL) was developed at the center. The foundation of this program was the view that if one learns to read and write in their native language, the acquisition of the second language will be easier. Women were the focus of this program, consisting of two thirds of the student population. Intergenerational participation was encouraged. Ligon (1995) reported that most wanted to learn to read and write in order to maintain contact with relatives and to maintain their culture and history through written works.

Similar to the concerns that were later voiced in the United States concerning bilingual education, Ligon (1995) reported that the use of "U. S. tax dollars to support the teaching of any language other than English was politically sensitive" (p. 94). The NLL program was scrutinized closely by those who were critical. The resounding theme from this program was that "literacy instruction can be more effective when teachers and students share a culture and language" (Ligon, 1995). Students were allowed to choose topics by posing questions on a bulletin board and had free access to a resource center. Teaching materials were translated into Iu-Mien and Hmong and parent-student handbooks were published in Iu-Mien and Hmong (Ligon, 1995).

Processing Center – Bataan, Philippines

The International Catholic Migration Commission administered the Philippine's Refugee Processing Center. In the late 1980s, the majority of young adults participating in the program were from Vietnam, with some families from Laos and Cambodia. A small percentage of the refugees were Iu-Mien. By the 1990s, the majority of young adults were Amerasians and their siblings who had experienced discrimination in their home country (Phillips, 1995). The majority of young children and elementary school aged children were Vietnamese (Hoyt, 1995).

With increased experience in the development of programs to prepare refugees for residing in the United States, innovative teaching methods were utilized. Following the Freirian method of problem-posing and the development of generative words, Wallerstein (1983) developed a curriculum for the ESL classes in the processing camp in 1982. Her belief was that programming should "encourage to develop self-confidence . . . [to] use their cultural and personal strengths to resolve problems"(p. 29). Wallerstein integrated her curriculum with a survival language program that was already in place by the Center for Applied Linguistics.

Burns (1991) related that as educators at the center became more aware of the political aspects of refugee assistance and the potential for "manipulation and exploitation for political or economic ends" (p. 66) of the refugees, they developed a program that "stress |ed| higher-level thinking skills" (p. 66). The educators provided programming to help students of all ages learn, viewing the "whole person" versus simply a student within the classroom, through problem-posing and "encouraging decisive action based on an awareness of the supports which American society provided" (p. 67).

Completion of the Overseas Program

The overseas programs came to a close in 1995. Due to what was viewed a success by its developers and those who implemented the programs, it became a model for U. S. Department of State funded programs in Croatia and Kenya (Ranard & Pfleger, 1995). The experiences gained led to a wealth of information on the teaching of second language learners.

The Southeast Asian Refugee Experience in the United States

Legislation Affecting Refugees Within the United States

The Indochina Migration and Refugee Assistance Act of 1975 (P.L. 94-23) provided federal reimbursement to the individual states for medical and cash assistance to refugees. This legislation was designed for one-time funding (Comeau, 1996). The result was the Reauthorization Act in 1977 that "continued federal funding and offered refugees the status of 'permanent resident'" (Comeau, 1996. p. 28). The Indochinese Refugee Children Assistance Act of 1976 reimbursed states for refugee children's education, including language instruction. It also funded adult refugee educational programs. It is important to note that many Americans felt apprehensive about the influx of Southeast Asian refugees. A public opinion poll in 1975, soon after the fall of Saigon, revealed that only 36% of those who responded were in favor of accepting refugees due to fears of increased public spending and job loss (University of California, Irvine, 2000).

The United States government chose to place refugees from Southeast Asian throughout the country in an effort to lessen the impact of the newcomers on communities (University of California, Irvine, 2000). Fadiman (1997) reiterated that this was a technique to encourage assimilation as well as a way to "avoid burdening any one community with more than its 'fair share' of refugees . . . " (p. 185). However, secondary migration occurred as clans reunited, with the majority of refugees moving to Texas and California. From 1975 to 1991, 993,300 refugees had arrived from Southeast Asia (University of California, Irvine, 2000).

The Refugee Act of 1980 (P.L. 96-212) institutionalized federal assistance and established the Office of Refugee Resettlement (ORR) in the Department of Health and Human Services. In order to receive the federal funding, each state had to develop a plan for serving refugees. In the United States, due to growing anti-welfare attitude, the public began to express concern over the high use of public assistance and low rate of securing employment by Southeast Asian refugees (Comeau, 1996; Tollefson, 1991). This attitude had a great impact on legislative funding for programs within the United States. Changes in programming shifted to less education with a greater focus on basic survival English. From 1987 to 1988, eligibility for special refugee assistance within the United States changed from three years to 12 to 18 months. Refugee educational programs ceased language and job training beyond basic survival levels needed to secure employment (Tollefson, 1991).

California Specific Refugee Assistance

A high percentage of refugees moved to California after initially settling in metropolitan areas throughout the United States. In response to the large number of Aid to Families with Dependent Children (AFDC) recipients, many of whom were refugees, California enacted in 1985 a unique program targeting training and employment of public assistance recipients. The Greater Avenues for Independence (GAIN) program focused on the securing of employment, but provided ESL and educational programs necessary for permanent employment. California developed the GAIN program to follow mandated properties of the federal Job Opportunity and Basic Skills (JOBS) training program. The federal JOBS program was replaced by the Temporary Assistance to Needy Families (TANF) in 1996. This legislation presented stricter federal guidelines for the participation in the program and limited the time receiving aid to 60 months in a recipient's lifetime. The focus was on the employment of aid recipients. This federal program led to GAIN changing to the California Work Opportunity and Responsibility to Kids (CalWORKS) program in 1998.

The percentage of Asians participating in the GAIN program in 1995-1996 was 11% (California State Job Training Coordinating Council, 2000). Information was not available from this source on the breakdown of Asian groups nor those who were limited English proficient.

Voluntary Agencies

The resettlement of refugees in the United States was successful, in part, because of voluntary agencies. Voluntary agencies (VOLAGS) were affiliated with various groups such as religious organizations, but all had the goal of helping the refugee become well adjusted to the new culture and become economically self-sufficient (Comeau, 1996). In 1975, VOLAGS began to get federal funding for refugee assistance. The International Rescue Committee, the United States Catholic Conference, and the Church World Service were a few of the many VOLAGS that helped with the initial needs of the refugees (University of California, Irvine, 2000).

Due to the overwhelming number of refugees entering the United States, the VOLAGS found that they needed additional help. Individual churches sponsored families. Relatives of refugees and Southeast Asian group within the United States were also recruited to sponsor incoming refugees, forming mutual assistance associations (Harmon, 1995; University of California, Irvine, 2000).

Entering the United States - The Beginning of Iu-Mien Communities

In 1978, the first groups of Iu-Mien refugees arrived in the United States. They were sponsored by churches in Seattle, Washington, Portland, Oregon, and San Francisco, California. The State Department of the United States reportedly was concerned about admitting "illiterate" refugees and thus, the first accepted for entrance into the United States were elite government officials and those who were considered literate (Habarad, 1987a; Ranard & Pfleger, 1993). These individuals reportedly were able to secure employment in a short period of time (Habarad, 1987a; Liegel, 1991).

It is estimated that almost a million refugees from Southeast Asia have settled in the United States since 1975 (Liegel, 1991). Following the "first wave" of refugees who were able to acculturate to the American society fairly rapidly, a second group beginning in 1979 experienced greater difficulty. This group was 33% less able to read and write in English than the previous groups. Many were described as being illiterate in their native language and unfamiliar with American culture since they had resided in the highlands of Laos, or were rural farmers or fisherman from Vietnam or Cambodia (Burns, 1991; Liegel, 1991). They experienced greater difficulty securing employment than the first group. By 1997, more than 32,000 Iu-Mien had resettled in the United States with the largest number (27,920) coming to California (MacDonald, 1997).

The Iu-Mien Experience in the United States

Upon arrival in the United States, refugees from the Iu-Mien community moved to locations near relatives or clan members. Soon after moving to the United States, 90% of Iu-Mien adults were unemployed (Habarad, 1987a) and most received Refugee Resettlement funds, Aid to Families with Dependent Children (AFDC), and Refugee Medical Assistance from Medicaid. With the changes in the national welfare program, frequently called "Welfare to Work" or "CalWORKS" in the State of California, the need to become trained and employable became a necessity for most who had been receiving public assistance. English language acquisition became a necessity for employment outside a family business.

Public Assistance For Refugees

In 1975, the United States government began a program to provide three years of public assistance along with language training for refugees (Ranard & Pfleger, 1993). The manner in which English was taught had included English immersion programs that focused on pronunciation versus communication (Ranard & Pfleger, 1993). The skills learned in these classes were not transferable to daily life. As related earlier, when more refugees began to flood camps in Thailand, language and cultural training became integrated in the classes. Training for the refugees then shifted to more practical knowledge of the language for use in the United States.

Current refugees now received less government assistance than previously, with funds available for a maximum of eight months (Ranard & Pfleger, 1995). Smith and Tarallo (1993) reported that the respondents in their study were "self-conscious" about receiving public assistance, but felt it was necessary for survival. This was especially true for the ones in their fifties and sixties who saw few employment opportunities because they had not acquired English language skills (Smith & Tarallo, 1993).

Many Iu-Mien refugees viewed receiving public assistance as a privilege and stayed within the law, relating that the abuses by others was upsetting (Smith & Tarallo, 1993). Refugees came from a collective culture that utilized the family and the village to help and thus some experienced conflict between the Southeast Asian culture of self-help and the Western welfare system (Comeau, 1996). Once refugees began arriving in 1975, Mutual Assistance Associations (MAA) were developed; they were organized and facilitated by refugees, replicating the collective help indicative of the culture.

The maze of the social welfare system in the United States presented great difficulty for many refugees. Weinstein-Shr (1994) provided an extensive study of the language problems that the Hmong experienced within the social welfare system, including difficulties with decoding government documents. For one of the participants in the study, "literacy skills are resources that enable him to take the role of culture broker" (Weinstein-Shr, 1994, p. 61). This individual was able to evaluate documents and important letters for the community and negotiate with social services to ensure other community members' needs were met.

Employment and Language

Smith and Tarallo (1993) provided a study of several groups of Iu-Mien residing in Sacramento, California. They noted that vocational skills from Lao and Thailand, such as blacksmithing, silver and goldsmithing, farming, and craftsmanship, were not transferable to the United States. In their study, two thirds of the respondents were unemployed (Smith & Tarallo, 1993). Those who were unemployed had an average educational level of 2.3 years in Laos, while the ones who were employed had five or more years of education. Two reportedly had graduated from high school; they would be considered "highly educated" in their home country. Pon (1984) related that many of "the lifeskills . . . were not transferable for life in America" (p. 3). This included the need to learn the use of coins and bills in the United States.

None of the unemployed in Smith and Tarallo's study (1993) spoke English and therefore, used others to translate in English. Only nine reported that they were able to understand "very little" English, and their spouses reportedly did not speak English either. Although most received public assistance, they related a desire to work. They had moved to Sacramento to be near family and receive English and vocational trainings that were reportedly not available in other parts of the United States.

The individuals in this study who were in their thirties and forties were in ESL classes with plans to transfer to vocational training programs in mechanics and machine work. They expressed a desire to work. However, the difficulty for many in securing employment had been the lack of English language skills (Habarad, 1987a; Smith & Tarallo, 1993).

One of Smith and Tarallo's (1993) findings was a noticeable difference between the employed and unemployed in regard to education and residing or working in rural or urban areas in Laos and/or Thailand. The employed were literate in Iu-Mien and several were described as literate in Laotian and Chinese. Many became fluent in Thai in the refugee camps. The employed were younger individuals and tended to be children of parents who traveled in their business in Laos, working in the lowland areas of Laos with exposure to "market language." Smith and Tarallo (1993) reported "they were able to transfer this advantage to new contexts in acquiring fluency in Thai and eventually English" (p. 115).

Habarad (1987a) revealed that fewer than 30 men of 3,000 in the Bay Area were employed three years after settlement. He stated that "most adults who could not yet read or write continued to enroll in training programs, often serially, but without seeking employment upon completion" (p. 81). A large percentage of the Iu-Mien participants had not written their spoken language and thus, "many learn [ed] to use pens and pencils for the first time in English-as-Second Language classes in the United States" (Chao, 1999, p. 2). It is important to note that many Iu-Mien men were literate in Chinese (Kandre, 1967, MacDonald, 1997), but this is not noted in the studies completed in the United States.

Strouse's (1989) study of the Hmong, another "closely-knit, agricultural, tribal people" (p. 3) of the highland of Laos, supported Chao's. It was noted that the schools in the United States did not educate the Hmong individuals for the types of jobs for which they might have transferable skills. The schools tend to focus on educating for college preparation, which can be difficult if one is not middle-class and college bound. American's labor market is very different from the rural areas of Laos and career exploration was needed.

Intergenerational Concerns

For the unemployed in the Smith and Tarallo (1993) study, "generational conflict with children appeared more pressing, and was the more frequently cited issue" (p. 111) than the issue of securing employment. Generational disenfranchisement occurred for many due to language barriers (Chao, 1999; Kang, Kuehn & Herrell, 1996; Smith & Tarallo, 1993). The parents cited problems in helping their children with schoolwork and communicating with the teachers who were not bilingual. Schools also lacked interpreters for assistance during parent conferences. Parents expressed feelings of helplessness addressing their children's behavior problems due to language barriers. One father stated, "When my daughter ran away from home, we reported to the police . . . we were unable to communicate with them due to the language" (Smith & Tarallo, 1993, p. 112).

In Chao's (1999) interviews with teenagers and their parents, the theme of generational conflict resounded, with parents having difficulty knowing their children's friends. This was a vast cultural difference and would be unheard of in the small enclaves in Laos where "parent-child relationships are more active in Iu-Mien culture than in Western cultures" (Chao, 1999, p. 5). Yaangh (2001) related that as Iu-Mien children adopt EuroAmerican culture such as a

> more direct American communication style, which includes: state your case, speak your mind, and tell me how you feel . . . they want to hear their parents say, "I love you; how are you feeling today?" Many of them feel their parents do not love them because they do not hear these words. (p. 4)

This transition from a high context culture, where community members are expected to infer emotions and meaning (Hall, 1997), to a low context culture where communication is explicit and detailed (Hall & Hall, 1990) can lead to miscommunication and frustration.

In addition to conflict in the family due to language barriers and differences in communication approaches, criminal activity has been a serious concern. Waters (1999) reported that the Iu-Mien youth have a much higher rate of commitment to the California Youth Authority than individuals from the Hmong community. For the males, ages 13 through 19 years, this rate is four times higher, with one in 35 being committed versus one in 130, respectively. The arrests were related to gang activity; the youth seem to be trying to assimilate into American culture while the elders "try to preserve the old life as much as possible" (Waters, 1999, p.19).

English as a Second Language (ESL) Programs

Simich-Dudgeon (1989) noted that refugees from Laos may be classified by some ESL/literacy programs as preliterate; they speak their native language and rely on an oral rather than written form of transmitting knowledge. Some refugees from Laos may have knowledge of writing in Chinese, but their English language acquisition was complicated by having to learn a new writing system upon immigration to the United States. Simich-Dudgeon (1989) related that "sociocultural differences and lack of prior literacy experiences further complicate their second language literacy acquisition" (p. 3).

Pon (1984) reported in his study that Vocational English as a Second Language (VESL) was part of the "Refugee Assistance Programs" through the United States Government and privately funded programs. The individuals who were entering these programs were unable to speak, read, or write in English. The focus of the programs then changed to basic ESL with lessons on "grammar, reading, writing and speaking" (Pon, 1984, p. 2). English was taught in the United States through immersion programs that focused on pronunciation versus communication (Ranard & Pfleger, 1993). The skills learned in these classes were not transferable to daily life.

Cultural and political differences of the various Southeast Asian groups were not recognized, and thus the relevance of English training for specifically the Iu-Mien and Hmong was ignored (Pon, 1984; Mingkwan, Kuehn, Baker, Le, Pen, Ricket, Rose, & Sananikone, 1995). Additionally, some programs lack cultural sensitivity. Mingkwan et al (1995) reported on teaching approaches that recognized English only in the classroom and specified communication activities that required the participants to sing or act out parts. These reportedly were seen as offensive to some of the students.

In the Smith and Tarallo study (1993), it appeared that the majority of those who did not take ESL classes or did not complete their course were over the age of fifty. However, when the researchers asked younger respondents their reasons for not attending classes, they cited having young children and planned to take classes when less involved in childcare. As Smith and Tarallo (1993) stated, "All of the employed respondents enrolled in ESL classes . . . tended to have youth on their side" (p. 123).

The findings were very significant in regard to the unemployed respondents who had been in the United States for nine or more years. It was found that during the time they had taken or were currently taking ESL classes, "not one . . . had a bilingual instructor or teacher's assistant who spoke Mien or Laotian" (Smith & Tarallo, 1993, p. 108). The recommendation from the Sacramento County assessment by Mingkwan, Kuehn, Baker, Le, Pen, Ricket, Rose, & Sananikone (1995) was that teaching assistants should be bilingual and that the teacher be a native English speaker.

The unemployed in the Smith and Tarallo (1993) reportedly were the individuals who were not fluent or did not have effective language skills in English. The authors stated, "Effective language training is particularly critical in the case of the Iu-Mien, who, of all the groups in our study, have traversed the greatest distances with regard to cultural traditions, work skills, and language structure" (Smith & Tarallo, 1993, p. 108). Additionally, Mingkwan et al (1995) noted that in Sacramento County, "teachers often encountered students with lack of cultural orientation training which impacts the ESL classroom" (p. 156). It is interesting that there appears to be a discrepancy between what was written about the classes in the United States regarding "cultural orientation" and literature cited previously that discussed cultural orientation classes provided in the refugee processing camps in Thailand and the Philippines. The camps were described as providing extensive training to prepare refugees for EuroAmerican culture (Liegel, 1991; Ranard & Pfleger, 1995).

In Strouse's (1989) study, it was noted that the curriculum for the Hmong adults was "not at all suitable for illiterates . . . did not take into account the enormous cultural gap . . . lacking sensitivity . . . to their poverty . . . " (p. 6). Childcare was difficult and affected the attendance of women in particular. For many Iu-Mien and other refugees from Laos, there was a collective experience of anxiety, depression, loss of self-esteem, and fear resulting from the traumas in Lao and refugee camps, and in adapting to the United States. Hemmendinger (1987) related that teachers needed to be aware of this and ensure "that the learners' lowest level of needs—physiological and safety—are met before they take classes" (p. 46). This included food, shelter and clothing, and working to build self-esteem and confidence. Mingkwan et al (1995) acknowledged that "appropriate diagnosis of and response to depression, other mental health problems, and learning disabilities can be complicated by the cross cultural context of adult refugee students in ELT classrooms" (p. 2).

Chapter 3

Cultural Aspects of the Iu-Mien People

In order to appreciate the needs of individuals from non-dominant groups, it is essential to be familiar with their background from a historical and cultural context. The foundation for an understanding involves insight into the subtle and complex aspects of sociohistorical experiences. This knowledge then aids in the comprehension of specific situations, such as the impact of Iu-Mien individuals' interactions with social workers.

As discussed below, the Iu-Mien people are considered transnational (MacDonald, 1997) and as a result, chose or were forced to live in many parts of Asia. The following discussion of the cultural aspects of the Iu-Mien people will focus on those who resided in the highlands of Laos and immigrated to the United States as refugees, beginning in 1978. Certain aspects of the Iu-Mien culture might be easily misunderstood by Westerners. An awareness of the different aspects of the culture is paramount in order to have insight into the areas of concern related by the participants in this study.

The majority of the information cited in this chapter was obtained from resources written by non-Iu-Mien individuals whose fields ranged from missionaries, refugee camp workers, educators, and health care workers. Thus, many of the perspectives come from one outside the Iu-Mien culture, and in turn, a Western lens may influence the subjective interpretations of rituals and beliefs.

One must be very careful when citing such material, due to concerns stated by Said (1978):

> . . . a large mass of writers . . . have accepted the basic distinction between East and West as the starting point for elaborate theories . . . social descriptions and political accounts concerning the Orient, its people, customs, mind, destiny, and so on . . . [and] Orientalism . . . [is] a Western style for dominating, restructuring, and having authority over the Orient. (p. 88)

Therefore, I feel the need to make a disclaimer to demonstrate awareness and sensitivity in providing this information. The view of the Iu-Mien culture, from an anthropological, sociological, and generally academic position, has primarily been documented in writings by Western, non-Iu-Mien, individuals. The information provided by individuals from the Iu-Mien community has manifested itself for the most part in the form of historical narratives in literary works, in Websites, unpublished handouts or papers, and public presentations. Additionally, from this recent evaluation, the majority of the written material has seemed to be generated by Iu-Mien women.

The Iu-Mien people are an important ethnic minority population in the history of Southeast Asia. Since they are such a small group, the amount of literature available is less than for other groups such as the Hmong, another highland group. However, what is written is quite detailed in many areas.

In this section, I present an overview of a culture that entails many intricate rituals and ceremonies. Because I am EuroAmerican, not Iu-Mien, I feel that I do not fully serve justice in this overview. I wish to portray a general picture of the culture that was maintained in Southeast Asia, prior to many individuals' immigration to the United States in the late 1970s. In some areas, I have described specific customs that have carried over into the United States.

The Iu-Mien's Migration History

The Iu-Mien people have moved from place to place for many centuries, from the central part of southern China to the hilltops of northern Laos and then, to the United States. The migration of the Iu-Mien people has been in response to and in conflict with the dominant society in the country and influences of outside countries.

The Iu-Mien people were initially from China. Sources vary as to how long they were there, with some saying as early as 1500 B.C. (Center for Applied Linguistics, 1981) or 2897 B.C.E. (Cross Cultural Health Care Program, 2000). The word "Mien" means "the people." For some, this is the term of preference as for centuries Southeast Asians and Chinese called the Iu-Mien people "Yao," which reportedly means "barbarian" (Moore-Howard, 1989, Saetern, 1998).

Many believe that "Yao" was a Chinese use of the "Iu" in Iu-Mien which was also spelled as "yu" and "yui" (MacDonald, 1997). However, the Iu-Mien in China continue to be referred to as Yao, and Yao is used in Laos and Thailand to refer to the Iu-Mien and others who speak the Yao language or dialects (Kandre, 1967). This can be quite confusing as there are Iu-Mien who speak dialects of Yao, yet call themselves Iu-Mien.

As the Chinese became more oppressive towards the Iu-Mien, small groups of Iu-Mien moved to the mountain areas of China, residing there until around the 1700s. At that time, they moved to northern Vietnam, Laos, Burma, and Thailand. Prior to World War II, the Iu-Mien population in Southeast Asia was estimated to be 150,000 to 200, 000. In Vietnam, the Iu-Mien people were called "Man" (Center for Applied Linguistics, 1981, p. 2), another word that meant "barbarian" The Iu-Mien people have maintained their culture with great resiliency through all the transitions to other societies. Waters (1990) related that the Iu-Mien culture was "developed in response to Chinese culture" (p. 135), utilizing parts of the Chinese culture such as language and Chinese characters as a form of assimilation, while maintaining unique features of the Iu-Mien culture. The Iu-Mien people are considered "essentially stateless...[as they] never had a specific national identity" (MacDonald, 1997, p.13). MacDonald (1997) viewed the Iu-Mien people as having a "transnational" (p. 14) identity since they have crossed national borders without being aligned with a specific nationality.

Clans and Family System

Clans

An Iu-Mien myth describes how the original 12 clans developed in China from a mistake in the planting of parts of a squash. The seeds of the squash were intended to be planted in the mountains, but were mistakenly planted in the valley. In turn, 12 pieces of squash (without the seeds) were sowed mistakenly in the mountains. These 12 pieces became the Iu-Mien people, with the seeds reproducing non-Iu-Mien in the valley. Because of this mistake, the Iu-Mien remained a small, minority population while those in the lowlands became the more dominant group.

Although there are 12 clans, the names vary from depending on the region or village (MacDonald, 1997). There are also subdivisions of the clans. The Iu-Mien people have a patrilineal descent pattern, clans inheriting membership from the father. The clan name is attached as surname and all individuals with the same surname are relatives, having a common ancestor.

Since there are relatively few clans, questions concerning one's lineage were reported by Kandre in 1967 as the most common interactions when individuals first meet. However, no clan seems to have greater status or power than another. Each clan has its own unique rituals for catching livestock or preparing foods (Lewis & Lewis, 1984).

The two branches of the Iu-Mien ethnic group that migrated to Southeast Asia from China were the Kim Mun of northern Vietnam, and the Iu-Mien of northern Laos and Thailand. McDonald (1997) states that the Man of Vietnam were the first to migrate outside of China possibly in the thirteenth century, but it is uncertain if MacDonald was referring to the Kim Mun or another branch. The Iu-Mien branch of the Yao migrated in the late 1700s.

In the United States, the naming pattern presents with the individual's given name first, followed by the surname. For registration in the refugee camps, Thai and Lao officials transposed Iu-Mien names to fit the pattern of the country they would resettle. The Thai word "Sae," (which originally came from the Chinese word meaning "clan name") (T. Waters, personal communication, November 6, 2000) indicated the Iu-Mien clan names. This became listed as part of the official Iu-Mien name. The "Sae" prefix was given to refugees who resided in camps in Thailand and intended to immigrate to the United States (Moore-Howard, 1989). Moore-Howard (1989) speculated that the prefix will be dropped over time and this was confirmed by my interview with Chao (2000) who related her husband dropped the "'Sae' and just kept the Chao because that is his original last name."

Clan names are listed below with the "Sae" prefix (Ask.com, 2000; Moore-Howard, 1989; Saetern, 2000). In conferring with K. Chao (personal communication, September, 22, 2000), there were reported disagreements among the Iu-Mien people as to how names are spelled and which names are truly Iu-Mien. K. Chao (personal communication, September, 22, 2000) related:

> The real pronunciation of the last names are very different...the shamans and spiritual priests read and wrote in Chinese characters because Mien itself is not a written language . . . the Chao last name is actually not Chao it is "Tzeo" or some loosely other spelling that sounds like that; it's more of each individual's perspective. And, when you interview any Mien, they will tell you something slightly different than the next.

As you can see from the list, there were more than twelve names uncovered in the research (Ask.com, 2000; Chao, 2000; Chao & Saechao, 2000; Moore-Howard, 1989; Mueke, 1983).

Saechao, Saechow, Saelau   Saechan or Saechin

Saetern or Saeturn or Saeteun or Saetang   Saedoh

Saelee   Saesai

Saephan or Saepharn or Saepan   Saelaw

Saeyang   Saedorngh

Saefong   Saeyongh

Saeshao   Saetong or Saethong

Saelio   Saelior

Saechin

Marriage and Marriage Ceremonies

Kandre (1967) described marriage as a "business transaction" (p. 593) that requires a transfer of wealth that will help ensure "success in life" (p. 493). This continues in the United States in the form of a "'Departure Fee' . . . payment of $2,000 to $4,000 . . . in both American dollars and silver" (MacDonald, 1997, p. 124). MacDonald (1997) related that the Iu-Mien people do not use the term bride price; however, several other Western and Iu-Mien writers have referred to this term. MacDonald's perspective was that a woman is not perceived as property of the husband; the monetary transaction is "meant to repay the family for the emotional loss of their daughter" (MacDonald, 1997, p.124). T. Waters (personal communication, November 6, 2000) related that, "an ideal fee is viewed as a symbol of the union between clans."

The perspective of marriage seems to vary in regard to the source describing the arrangement. M. L. Saechao (1999), when discussing marriage in the United States related, "men have to buy their wives with a dowry . . . it is like being treated like an item in a store" (p. 8). Additionally, F. L. Saechao (1999b) stated, "because money is such an important factor in determining how much respect your family receives, daughters are often married off to the highest bidder" (p.18). She compared marriages in the United States to Laos and the impact of the EuroAmerican value system on the traditional Iu-Mien culture. She stated,

> I'm very happy to be living here in America instead of the motherland. I
> don't have to "learn " to love my husband before or after I marry him. I
> don't have to marry someone my mother and father chose to me. Most
> important of all . . . I don't have to marry my husband's family, but him
> alone. (p. 18)

Traditionally, once married, the bride resides with her husband's family, which may include his parents, siblings, and elders. She is responsible for the care of the family.

In traditional Iu-Mien families, the oldest sons and daughters must marry first, followed by their respective younger siblings (MacDonald, 1997). This order is considered very important. An Iu-Mien person may marry someone with the same surname as long as they are not patrilineally related within three generations (MacDonald, 1997; Moore-Howard, 1989). Marriage can occur if there is a matrilineal relationship within three generations. This further requirement reinforces the patrilineal descent pattern of the Iu-Mien people.

Boys and girls may marry whom they want as long as they have compatible birth dates (Lewis & Lewis, 1984, MacDonald, 1997). The groom's parents may send a representative to the potential bride's home to assess if there is an affinity of birthdates by the Chinese calendar (Chao & Saechao, 1999). When a couple desires to marry, they must consult an astrologer to select the most favorable time for the wedding. The time may be at any point in the day or night, such as one or two o'clock in the morning.

MacDonald (1997) stated that the marriage custom of the Iu-Mien people in both Laos and the United States dictates that one is not to marry until age 18. However, he noted that a person who is not married by the time they are 18 is thought to be "selfish and unwanted" (p. 121). M. L. Saechao (1999) related that the teen years are "when most parents believe their daughters are ready for marriage" (p. 8) and that sons are not pressured to marry as early.

In Laos, if a young woman has a suitor, he may come to her bedroom. In Laos and the United States it is not uncommon for children to be born prior to marriage. Nonmarital births are not a source of stigma in the Iu-Mien culture. Traditional Iu-Mien stories allude to nonmarital sex. An example of this is in *The Trials of the Orphan Brothers* (Saechao, L. C., 1993): "they told the brothers to choose the girl they wanted to sleep with . . . " (p. 580).

The custom of premarital sex has continued in the United States. One Oregon leader estimated that approximately 50% of Iu-Mien high school girls were pregnant before graduating (MacDonald, 1997). It was not noted by this source how many were married at the time of pregnancy.

Traditional Iu-Mien weddings are broken into major or minor, depending on the financial status. The major wedding lasts three days, while a minor will last only one day (MacDonald, 1997). In Laos, the trend is for a one-day wedding due to the great expense. In the United States, families have more money and three-day weddings provide an opportunity for the groom's family to "display its prosperity" (MacDonald, 1997, p. 127).

In the film, *Kelly Loves Tony* (Nakasako, 1998), Kelly described her engagement in the United States: "I didn't even know I was engaged. I came home from school and saw his parents leaving . . . I saw all this food . . . Mom showed me the silver bracelets and told me I was engaged." Traditionally, an engagement dinner occurs in the girl's home, a rooster is killed, and the groom's family gives silver bracelets for the engagement. If it is decided that the couple will marry, another engagement dinner is arranged to discuss the dowry and the number of pigs to be killed for the ceremony (Chao & Saechao, 1999).

In Laos, it is best if a couple becomes engaged after the rice harvest, in the winter. This then allows the girl a year to sew and embroider outfits for herself and her husband, pants for her mother-in-law, and neck edgings for all her aunts and sisters-in-law (Fong & Saeteun, 1989). She is not required to work in the fields during this time in order to complete all the outfits. In the United States, frequently the outfits are purchased from Thailand. The two families may then divide the cost. The changing role of traditional clothing is exemplified by Takaki's (1998) quote of an Iu-Mien parent:

> [The mother stated] "we only wear our traditional clothing on special days, and I will make my children only one set of clothes. When they grow up I don't know if they will marry American or Mien, so I will make only one set." (p. 466)

The day before the wedding, the groom's family meets with the bride's in her home. A bride price and/or dowry are exchanged and a meal shared. The maternal uncle or the husband of the bride's next older sister oversees the payment. It is during this time that a ceremony is performed to inform the bride's house spirits that she will be moving and that she no longer needs to be protected in her parent's home. The night prior to the wedding, she then stays at a relative's or friend's home.

During the wedding ceremony, the bride may wear two pairs of pants and two jackets, one being made by the bride and one by her mother-in-law. In major ceremonies, she may wear an elaborate headdress. The bride, in her new home, participates in a ceremony with the priest to alert the house spirits to a new family member. Her bags are opened to let out "all evil spirits" (Fong & Saeteun, 1989, p. 3).

A face washing ceremony follows in which a bowl and cup of water is draped with a set of chopsticks and a Chinese towel. The bowl is offered first to men in a specific order, and then lastly, to the women. Once the person who is offered the opportunity to wash performs a ceremonial gesture, the cup is emptied of water, and money is placed in it. The towel is kept as a gift. In Laos, the water is collected and thrown under the groom's bed. In the United States, it may be collected for a few days in a bucket or immediately thrown away (Fong & Saeteun, 1989). Following the entire wedding ceremony, which may include rituals such as a bowing ceremony by the groom (Gogol, 1996; Houghton, 1989), the bride cooks a meal for the entire family, signifying she is a married woman.

In the United States, families may hire a band and the couple may share a traditional American wedding cake. A large public luncheon may be provided for the bride and groom's family and friends. During the luncheon, a tea ceremony is performed and monies are provided to the bride during this ceremony.

Children and Naming System

Children are viewed as flower spirits and the spirits of their ancestors are their guardians. Mothers, during pregnancy, make a special hat for the baby that is decorated with bright red pompoms, embroidery, beads, and bells. The child wears his or her hat during childhood. At adolescence, a ceremony is performed to alert the flower spirits that they may now leave. The ancestors are then informed that the child has become an adult.

Children in Laos are born at home. However, for nonmarital births, the mother gives birth in a hut built next to the house (Houghton, 1989). Children are greatly loved, thus the lack of stigma over premarital childbirth. A couple is expected to have a child by the time they have been married three years. If spirit worship does not work and a child is not born within five years, a child will be adopted (MacDonald, 1997). Iu-Mien children may only be adopted by other Iu-Mien families. However, children may be adopted from other groups such as the Lao. Lewis and Lewis (1984) told of a couple that had eight biological children, and also adopted ten additional children from other ethnic groups.

Due to the belief in reincarnation, there is no stigma towards adoption; an ancestral spirit may have chosen the adoptee to become part of the family (MacDonald, 1997). In some cases, entire families who are not Iu-Mien may be adopted into a village, "taking on the Iu-Mien ethnic identity" (MacDonald, 1997, p. 43). Kandre (1967) related in his study that 10% of the population had been "purchased" (p. 594) from various groups such as the Lao, Thai, and Lahu. Most were young children at the time they entered the Iu-Mien community.

Children are named depending on their birth order, which follows the Chinese number system. (Lewis & Lewis, 1984). Boys are given a Chinese number to indicate position in the family in regard to birth order and their father's name. For example, San Chao means third son of Mr. Chao. The numbering system is as follows:

Lao Ta – first son

Lao Le – second son

Lao San – third son

Additionally, a son will receive a "'small name' which uses the second part of the father's name for the second part of each child's name" (Lewis & Lewis, 1984, p. 156). The names are as follows:

First son - the first syllable will be Kao or Ton

Nai – second son

San or Son – third son

Su or Sou – fourth son

Ou or Lou – fifth son

Chee – sixth son

Pa – seventh son

Cheo - eighth son

Shiep or Chiep (ninth son)

Lai or Chai (last child)

Boys receive a generational name that he shares with his brothers and male cousins. They are also given an individual or official name that later becomes his children's family name. At the age of 12, the biological father gives his son a ceremonial name, that is, a spirit name. This name is to be used by the children of the boy after his death when they pray to him or make offerings.

Female babies are given an Iu-Mien number to designate their position in relation to other daughters. They are also given their father's individual name. The numbering of girls is as follows:

May or Mey – first daughter

Nai – second daughter

Fam, Farm, or Fahm– third daughter

Fay, Faye, Feuy, or Femy – fourth daughter

May or Manh – fifth daughter

Lai - sixth daughter

Chet – seventh daughter

Pet – eighth daughter

Chua – ninth daughter

Tsiep – tenth daughter

Chai or Lai (last child)

The girl's names are followed by the second name of the father. They are given their spirit name after they are married (Saetern, 2000). For example, Fay Chao means the fourth daughter of Mr. Chao.

Children may be given a nickname due to circumstances of the birth. If a child becomes ill, their name may be changed as the initial name is viewed as being the wrong one for the child to begin with. Examples of names given due to special circumstances include:

Chen, Cheng, or Seng ("to help," umbilical cord wrapped around neck of baby)

Kea (guest came into house while baby was being born)

Lien (born in shelter in Thailand)

Chan (problems with birthing)

Koy ("turn around"), Yian ("change"), and Gen ("place in-between") are names given if a family has a large amount of girls. The names are given in the hopes that the next child will be a boy (Chao & Saechao, 2000).

Roles in the Family

In the Iu-Mien culture, family is considered the "most important social unit" (Lewis & Lewis, 1984, p. 26). Each member of the family unit is regarded as having an important role, with the elders being the most highly respected. The gender roles are described as being "more strict for females" (Saechao, M. L., 1999). The married son and wife have major roles within the family unit. A family frequently consists of a husband and his wife, their unmarried children, their married son's wife (or wives), and their children. It is not uncommon to have 20 people living in a family unit and there may be as many as 60 people residing in a household (Lewis & Lewis, 1984).

In Iu-Mien families, individuals are addressed by their role in the family and in accordance with their relationship to others by age. Yaangh (2001) noted that if he was interviewing an adult male father who was older than he, he would address the individual as "older brother." The man's wife would be called "sister-in-law." The manner of addressing is very important as a violation of this norm would cause the person to "be considered ignorant and prideful . . . he will not be respected and [will be] 'looked down' upon by other Mien" (Yaangh, 2001, p. 22).

Men

Iu-Mien culture is patrilineal and patrilocal. Men hold greater power than women. This is exemplified by the custom that men are fed first. Men are responsible for hard labor such as cutting trees, though they work in the fields with women. In the United States, Mey Liam Saechao (1999) related, "many Iu Mien men expect a hot meal, a clean house and an obedient wife when they come home" (p.9).

Women

Women are primarily responsible for the care of the children and home, and the making of clothing. Women are not allowed to eat with the men and accordingly, eat at a different table. They are responsible for serving during ceremonies and preparing tea or coffee for guests (Saechao, M. L., 1999). Women are considered subservient to men. In Laos, they spend the majority of their waking hours in the kitchen or working in the fields. The role of women has changed some since coming to the United States. Young Iu-Mien women in the United States are experiencing conflict with their elders as M. L. Saechao (1999)ˑ described:

> Some parents, like mine (especially my father), don't understand why people like myself don't want to accept and can't understand this tradition [or respecting elders]; it leads to arguments and I'm considered disrespectful. We're not allowed to say what we think is right . . . being a Iu Mien girl is hard. We are treated unfairly. (p.9)

Traditional roles may tend to prevail, but young adult Iu-Mien women in the United States are attending college. Though they may live with their in-laws, the family helps to care for their children while they attend school (Chao, 2000; Nakasako, 1998).

Children

In Laos, children are taught to work and participate in the family chores at a young age. Girls learn to embroider as early as age four (Moore-Howard, 1989). Work within the home is gender specific beginning from birth; girls learn home care tasks while boys may learn to hunt, read, and write. Boys remain with their family of origin, in the family home when they marry, while girls move in with the family they marry into. This custom has continued in the United States.

In traditional Iu-Mien families, parent-child communication is for the purpose of ensuring children obey their parents. Yaangh (2001) related that the interactions tend to "revolve around do's and don't . . . to obey the rules established by the parents" (p. 4). The belief is that actions, not words, display the love of a parent and visa versa.

Elders

Elders are provided "special respect . . . [because they] know a great deal ... [thus, the] younger generation should listen to them" (Lewis & Lewis, 1984,

p. 151). The life expectancy of a Iu-Mien individual in Laos is 60 years and thus, birthdays are only recorded to age 60 (Cross Cultural Health Care Program, 2000). Within the United States, elders have experienced the greatest difficulty due to isolation from lack of English language skills, transferable employment skills, and traditional values in a changing family system. Depression is not uncommon and "many elders are virtual prisoners in their own home, unable even to answer the phone or the door" (Vuong & Huynh, 1992, p. 21).

Domestic Violence

Domestic violence in the Iu-Mien community is rarely discussed in the literature. It is anonymously addressed in the literary journal, *Quality Torn* (Anon., 1999). The writer, who resides in the United States, described incidents of physical abuse sustained by her mother, herself, and her siblings at the hands of her stepfather.

> My mother was like a walking and talking dummy that was controlled by a monster that lived in the house with us . . . I know that these abuses happen in the Iu Mien community . . . but not many of the women want to talk about it because they're all scared. People in the community add to the problem by gossiping and exaggerating. (Anon., 1999, pp. 14-15)

Y. W. Saechao (1999a) talked of her childhood friend whose mother would beat her. She stated, "I thought her parents should treat her right before doing anything else to her. In a way I felt bad because it wasn't my business . . . but I just couldn't stand it" (Saechao,Y. W. 1999a, p. 16).

Values, Spirituality, and Ceremonies

Values

The Iu-Mien ideology focuses on cooperation and harmony with the natural and spirit world. Central themes include a respect for money, intelligence, and merit-making for the spirit world. An individual and a family do not want to lose face and thus, "institutionalized politeness" (Kandre, 1967, p. 587) is a prevailing force in diffusing conflicts and maintaining peace. Proscriptive norms include not interrupting older speakers and not speaking out loudly or demanding that one's own way be followed (Houghton, 1989). The Iu-Mien people are described as being "slow to anger" (Moore-Howard, 1989, p. 21). Kandre (1967) related the belief that if one quarrels, that is, unable to cooperate, they will then become weak and in turn, make less money.

The Iu-Mien's primary cultural theme is desire for propriety. Hence, they are described as a dignified people (Chao & Saechao, 1999; Lewis & Lewis, 1984). Lewis and Lewis (1984) stated that the Iu-Mien "prize decorum highly . . . [and] desire to avoid open conflict at all costs . . . seeking to resolve the problem before it blocks their joint pursuit of merit and status" (p. 10). Flexibility in addressing concerns is common to avoid conflicts (Houghton, 1989; Moore-Howard, 1989). If family members are unable to resolve a conflict, one will be asked to move out in order to avoid further problems (Kandre, 1967).

In Laos, silver in the form of French Indochinese coins is the primary form of currency and the more silver, the more successful a person. This is reinforced by the belief that life is dependent on the continual accumulation of silver (Kandre, 1967). Silver is also the medium to the spirit world. The Iu-Mien people are described as having a preoccupation with money (Moore-Howard, 1989). However, this is not seen in a negative light, rather, the focus on money and silver is an integral part of the deep value for family, elders, and a respectful life (Kandre, 1967; Moore-Howard, 1989). This will be discussed in greater depth in terms of spirituality.

Spirituality

One of the most important aspects of traditional Iu-Mien culture is their spiritual beliefs. The Iu-Mien people place a high value on ancestor worship. Many are animists who worship the spirits of nature as well as those of their departed ancestors. This belief entails the view that "natural objects . . . all possess souls or a life-force" (Houghton, 1989, p. 25). The ancestors from the previous four generations are most revered. They are alerted to the important events in the home such as a birth of a child, marriage, or other new family members. The ancestors are viewed as helping, in practical ways, the living relatives (Houghton, 1989). Many Iu-Mien people believe in reincarnation or rebirth. For example, an individual may be reincarnated to pay back a large debt from a previous life (Lewis & Lewis, 1984).

Families have maintained written records of their ancestors which include the offerings of spirit money, silver and gold, ceremonies held for the ancestor, and the location of their burial site (Habarad, 1987b; Saetern, 2000). These records are passed on through the male line, and copies are made for family members that move. Habarad (1987b) related viewing such a record that dated back 15 generations.

Spirits

Kandre (1967) reported that "the Iu-Mien operate on two levels of existence: the world of men (jaang keen) and the world of spirits (jom keen)" (p. 596). The bridge to these worlds is through silver. The spirit world is very complex, consisting of spirits in all aspects of life, residing in homes and the outside world as well as manifesting many forms and types (Houghton, 1989). Spirits are believed to be stupid, believing "everything the shaman says" (Moore-Howard, 1989, p. 39) such as paper, that is made to look like money, is actually silver. The spirits are described as liking silver because it is considered pure like the heavens (McDonald, 1997).

The spirits greatly "dislike sexual intercourse" (Kandre, 1967, p. 597) because it is considered impure. Men are the only ones allowed to worship spirits because women are considered impure; they menstruate and give birth to children. This view of women requires men not to have sexual relations for a certain time before and after a ritual, and for women only to be able to gain a spiritual place indirectly through their husbands and sons (MacDonald, 1997). Women are able to only fully participate in few rituals. However, they do prepare food for the rituals. The role of women has changed somewhat since immigrating to the United States. This is discussed in greater detail in the area on roles in the family.

The spirits reside in a world that is opposite to humans. This opposite world includes the spirits working at night and being weak, unlike humans who are considered strong. The Iu-Mien people believe in maintaining a good relationship with the spirits in order not to anger them, and in turn, cause illness. Spirits are viewed as controllable through gifts, sacrifices, and pledges of allegiance (Houghton, 1989). They do, however, have a "spirit government that controls events both in the spirit world and the world of men" (Houghton, 1989, p. 72). The Iu-Mien people do not build temples, but make spirit houses (altars) to feed and honor the spirits.

L. C. Saechao (1999) stated that in the United States, spirits may be asked to help with problems such as:

> . . . if someone steals our car and we want to know where it's (sic) been or who took it, we'll ask the spirits. They won't give us a specific answer, though. They'll say it's nearby, or there's nothing wrong with it, or it'll be back in five days. (p. 26)

Houghton (1989) related that a Iu-Mien individual who was source for his research stated that when the Iu-Mien people moved to the United States they searched for the regional spirit. They "discovered that the American Indian spirit was in charge, and some tried to worship it" (Houghton, 1989, pp. 107 -108).

Souls

Each person has many souls that are located in different parts of the body, including "three in the head and seven in the legs." (Lewis & Lewis, 1984, p.156). A person will become sick if one of the souls leaves the head. If all the souls leave the body, a person will die. Souls are viewed as being easily dislodged from the body, and Houghton (1989) related that one may be fearful of sudden movement because of this possibility. The souls in children are seen as becoming frightened easily (Houghton, 1989).

Souls of the ancestors need money, food, clothing, and houses for survival. Spirit money for the spiritual world is paper that has been stamped using a very wet ink to provide an embossed impression. Saetern (2000) described that spirit money may be made by hammering special paper with "Chinese 'chop' marks carved on the end of a piece of buffalo horn" (p. 1). In Laos, the paper was made out of bamboo; in the United States, many use brown, institutional type, paper towels. The spirit money is burned, and in this process, becomes actual money in the spirit's world. Paper that is stamped with designs of Gods and horses is burned so that a person's souls in heaven will have money and horses to provide assistance (Saechao, L. C., 1999).

Taoism

In addition to belief in spirits and ancestors, many Iu-Mien people believe in Taoism. Scholars believe that the Iu-Mien people gained this religious belief from life in China five to six centuries ago (Lewis & Lewis, 1984; MacDonald, 1997; Moore-Howard, 1989). It is very expensive to follow the rituals correctly. Expenses include the cost of an individual who is able to read the texts that are in Chinese (Lewis & Lewis, 1984) and religious leaders who can perform the ceremonies. Additionally, there are livestock and other essentials needed to perform a ceremony.

The Taoist pantheon, the celestial hierarchy that includes the supreme functionaries, are painted in a set of 17 pictures. The process in which these are painted is quite elaborate. The painter must be in a setting that is religiously pure, and during the several months that it takes to paint them, the client and the painter must be celibate (Lewis & Lewis, 1984). Additionally, a long scroll accompanies the pictures, hanging above them during ceremonies. The scroll may be placed about the "Big Door" in the home (described later in this chapter), and may be as long as 2.5 meters or more (Lewis & Lewis, 1984). Other smaller pictures hang with the 17. The scrolls are rolled and stored in a special bag, and thus can be easily carried when the family moves (MacDonald, 1997). The scrolls are only displayed during specific rituals.

Priests

Priests learn their practice from other priests, with powers being passed on through families. MacDonald (1997) related that the role of priest is "the closest to a privileged class" (p. 49) in the Iu-Mien culture. They are described as having skill in communicating with the spirit world, performing ceremonies involving the Taoist pantheon, and being literate in Chinese. Priests can accumulate wealth by performing rituals. Their primary role is to "preside over the ritual life of the village" (Houghton, 1989, p. 113). Their communication with the spirits "is strictly regulated by written manuals that carefully prescribe the order of the liturgy" (Houghton, 1989, p. 130).

Shamans

Shamans are men who are believed to have inherited their abilities to be possessed by supernatural beings or are chosen by spirits to be a medium. There are two types of Shamans. The Shaman with the greater power is able to work with spirits above the sky, while a lesser Shaman focuses on the small spirits who reside below the sky (Lewis & Lewis, 1984; Moore-Howard, 1989). They have a very special role in contacting the world of spirits through spirit possession or in a trance as a medium (Houghton, 1989).

The Shaman's primary role is to help those who are sick through curing ceremonies (Houghton, 1989; Lewis & Lewis, 1984). Spirits may invade the body and thus "curing rituals are necessary" (Schultz, 1982, p. 153). In curing ceremonies, the patient may not have been seen by the Shaman. The Shaman has no physical contact with the person in need and herbal medicine may be used. Specific protocols, which are quite elaborate, are followed. These may include collecting blood from a sacrificed pig or the use of a divining stick to question ancestors and spirits.

Christianity

Christian missionaries in Southeast Asia were met with some resistance by the Iu-Mien people who viewed the conversion as synonymous with losing their Iu-Mien identity (MacDonald, 1997). In the United States, some Iu-Mien individuals have voiced concern over the loss of the Iu-Mien culture due to conversion to Christianity. Others have related that they converted due to the simplicity and ease in "turn[ing] to Jesus as a superior being who will overpower the angry ancestors and solve their problems" (MacDonald, 1997, p. 171). These problems might include illness or an unexpected experience that seems unrelated to anything save bad luck. Additionally, conversion may be also influenced by the fact that there are less monetary costs involved in the Christian religion. The spiritual beliefs that include ancestor worship and merit-making ceremonies required forms of wealth to support the ceremonies.

Habarad (1987b) related that conversion to Christianity might be viewed as a strategy to maintain relationships while escaping the powerful nature of the ancestor spirits. Houghton (1989) substantiated this by stating that one of his sources related that the primary reason for conversion is to "escape from fear of the spirits" (p. 183) who dominate their lives. He shared a story of a Iu-Mien convert in the hills of Laos who stated to a Western visitor who was disappointed that the village was not left untouched by missionaries, "'before I lived in constant fear of the spirits. I was always worried. Now I have peace because of Jesus'" (Houghton, 1989, p. 225).

Some Iu-Mien converts to Christianity have believed that they should destroy all of the Iu-Mien books. Others have focused on the spirit-related texts, saving the historical sources. Sacred objects have been destroyed or sold, including the set of the 17 pictures of the Taoist pantheon (MacDonald, 1997).

In the United States, Portland, Oregon, has one of the largest number of Christians in the Iu-Mien community; Christians make up at least 40% percent of the community (MacDonald, 1997). Chinn (2000) related that in the United States approximately 4,200 "Iu-Mienh" (Chinn, 2000) are Christian. Conversion to Christianity has caused turmoil in some families, especially when children convert without asking permission of their parents. The greatest concern is that

> the convert no longer feels obliged to help his or her deceased parents. . . [is not involved in] thanking and paying the ancestors who gave the child life . . . [he or she] now thanks the Christians who the Taoist do not think have given anything. (MacDonald, 1997, p. 213)

However, for others whose parents converted and raised their families in the United States as Christian, becoming a Christian is viewed as a pivotal point in their life. (Saephan, 1999). Churches that provided sponsorship to the United States are seen in a positive light as one young woman related, they "helped me learn English . . . [and] adjust to America every step of the way" (Saechao, Y. W., 1999b, p. 29). Chinn (2000) stated, "many believe that it is by God's grace that they have come to the United States, the 'land of opportunity'" (p. 5). He viewed the church as a forum for maintaining the Mienh community through the socializing that occurs during church services and activities.

Holidays and Ceremonies

New Year

Iu-Mien families traditionally maintain a written record of their ancestors that "follows the course of their souls and spirits in the after-life spirit world . . . [and the families keep a] record of specific symbolic offerings of silver, gold, and paper money provided to each ancestor's spiriting, prioritised (sic) by importance" (Saetern, 2000, p. 1). Three to five days before the New Year, spirit money is placed on the floor in front of the spirit altar in the house. The money is then burned, with the offering going up to the spirit world in the smoke. The New

Year celebration in Laos is described as a time for "feasting and romantic liaisons for the young people . . . [they] walk in procession to every house in the village to exchange and receive blessings of the elders" (Saetern, 2000, p. 1). During the 1960s, the CIA provided money for the New Year celebrations, and public traditional dancing became part of the process (MacDonald, 1997).

New Year celebrations continue in the United States. Some Iu-Mien communities have invited the public to join in the celebration. These are in contrast to the more private ceremonies in Laos. This has helped to bridge the Iu-Mien and EuroAmerican communities (Chao & Saechao, 2000). In the United States, red dyed eggs are given to children who may pass them on to friends and teachers (Fong & Saeteun, 1989). Additionally, spirit money is burned to alert the ancestors to the ending of the year. New Year is considered a time to settle old debts (Fong & Saeteun, 1989).

Merit-Making Ceremonies

The Iu-Mien people are unique from other Southeast Asian cultures in regard to the Iu-Mien participation in merit-making ceremonies (Habarad, 1987b; Lewis & Lewis, 1984). These ceremonies focus on bridging the two worlds of man and spirits. The goal of the ceremony is to gain respect in the spirit world for current success and success for a man's family when he dies (Kandre, 1967). For example, the "Hanging the Lanterns" ceremony is a beginning rite to introduce boys, before they are 20, to the Taoist pantheon. The two or three day ceremony designates a boy as a true Iu-Mien, and guarantees him "entry into the realm of the ancestors when he dies" (Lewis & Lewis, 1984, p. 160). Habarad (1987b) described the boy entering into the initiating ceremony in women's clothes, leaving dressed as a man which is viewed as a "symbolic transformation from child to woman to man through immersion in supernatural knowledge" (p. 63).

Men are promoted later in life though a ceremony that designates a special name signifying a higher status. During the ceremony, women attend and "share in their husband's promotion" (Lewis & Lewis, 1984, p. 160). These merit-making ceremonies can be very expensive and thus, many men may participate in one ceremony to share expense (Lewis & Lewis, 1984). The spiritual name that is given follows the clan name, and the men may have as many as three different levels of the spirit names (Saetern, 2000).

Death

Specific ceremonies occur following the death of a Iu-Mien group member, including a ceremony to confirm the identity of the loved one in order for their soul to go to heaven (Saetern, 2000). L. C. Saechao (1999) related that if a ceremony is not held, the person's soul will remain in the body and "it will be lost . . . it will find its way back to where it used to live and haunt its own family" (p.26). Pigs are killed and the family ceremony lasts for at least two days. The spirits are believed to be smell the cooked meat and then become nourished (Saechao, L. C., 1999).

The worshiping of ancestors is told in traditional stories such as "The Yiem-Fiu Mien and The Orphan" (Saephan, 1995). An unmarried sister died and was not worshiped by the family. In this morality tale, it is not until the older brother utilized a shaman to help open the "bridge between life and death" that the family "became prosperous and respected . . . never worried about money again . . . " (Seaphan, 1995, p. 32).

The death rituals end with a cremation, following a burial of the ashes 24 hours later by a male relative and priest. The burial spot is determined by divining sticks (Lewis & Lewis, 1984), or by testing the prospective area with an uncooked egg. The egg is thrown up and if, when it hits the ground, it does not break, which reportedly happens on a frequent basis, then other burial spots must be evaluated until the egg breaks (Saetern, 2000).

A grave needs to be favorably located so that the "ancestor's spirit will be respected by all other spirits, regardless of rank . . . [and] descendants born will be protected against attacks of bad spirits . . . [and that they] will be clever and rich"

(Kandre, 1967, p. 613). MacDonald (1997) related that gravesites must be located high on a hill in order to be near a group of outdoor spirits.

In the United States, the belief in the spirit world has continued for many, particularly the elderly. Habarad (1987b) related that ancestral obligations that are not met are seen as placing "all within the community at risk of incurring supernatural wrath" (p. 154). He described the unexpected death of two men two months after a ceremony. These deaths were viewed by the Northern California Iu-Mien community as a result of a "violation of the prohibitions surrounding the regional ceremony . . . " and were seen as a "public rebuke to men and women suspected of no longer taking their obligations seriously" (p. 157).

The traditions from Laos have been maintained in the United States by elders and some of the 1.5 generation, those who were born outside the United States, but came to the United States prior to adolescence. L. C. Saechao (1999) stated,

> I didn't know much about my religion or culture until I asked my Parents . . . to me, having these beliefs mean good luck and a good life. I strongly believe that our ancestors are right beside us, guiding . . . if I didn't believe in them, I wouldn't be able to find things in life. (p. 27)

Government and Social Systems

Role of the Headman

The Iu-Mien, as a transnational people, have maintained values that support adjustment "to local government requirements and . . . [thus work] to live acceptably within the prevailing social system" (Lewis & Lewis, 1984, p. 169). Village headmen are appointed for social control and also are required to attend village celebrations. A headman may be a person from another village, a person of privilege and wealth that has "good ancestry" (MacDonald, 1997, p. 49). The headman is described as a leader whose job is not to judge, but to suggest ways to resolve issues in a fashion that is quick, mutually accepted, and as comfortable as possible for all involved. Overall, he is responsible for the welfare of the village and represents it in outside dealings (Houghton, 1989).

The headman presides over formal proceedings, using subtle pressure for offenders to conform. Expulsion from a village is seen as the last possible resolution (Kandre, 1967). It is important to note that "the main principle of the lu-Mien judicial system is not revenge, but to repair damage to individuals" (Kandre, 1967, p. 602). The community seeks "reparation for damage and restoration of the smooth functioning of the social interactions . . . " (Kandre, 1967, p. 603). The headman may settle a dispute by fining the offending party (Moore-Howard, 1989). Houghton (1989) related that the headman is considered the final authority and his decisions are absolute. Houghton (1989) described the use of fines to settle disputes and beatings for serious offenses. For deviant crimes, such as child molestation, the offender may be forced to crouch on his hands and knees to eat grass. This reportedly is viewed as a form of shame, reducing the offender to the animal like state he exhibited in his behavior, and/or is seen as a way to force vomiting that "will cause the evil spirit to be cast out" (Houghton, 1989, p. 94).

Social Control and Values

Wealth and Power

Wealth, for men, is considered an indicator of freedom. Those with wealth may be able to dispute laws or commit a crime without great social and legal recourse. Moore-Howard (1989) noted, "one has to be rich to get away with murder without extremely serious consequences for oneself. For this reason, rich men are feared" (p. 22). Rich men have the ability to pay a compensation for crimes they may have committed (Kandre, 1967; MacDonald, 1997; Moore-Howard, 1989).

Harmony

The Iu-Mien culture greatly values harmony. Thus, if there is a problem in a family and it does not seem to resolve, one of the quarreling members will move out to avoid further problems (MacDonald, 1997; Moore-Howard, 1989). Harmony is a central theme in all interactions and focuses on the collective and long-term implications. Kandre (1967) noted that if a contract is breached, the community is informed and the offender loses face until he is able to honor his obligations, that is, until he is able to "'wash his face'" (p. 602).

Villages and Houses

Villages in Laos are located along streambeds in the highlands or on mountain ridges (T. Waters, personal communication, November 6, 2000) approximately "1,650 to 3,650 feet above sea level" (MacDonald, 1997, p. 40). The villages consist of ten to 100 hundred individuals with an average of 15 homes grouped by clan. There may be two or more clans in a village with one frequently larger than the others represented in the village. Kandre (1967) related that "the village is merely an aggregate of the household" (p. 600).

Families may stay in a village from ten to 15 years. Smaller villages tend to move more often than villages consisting of many people. Villages are frequently located within a day's journey from other Iu-Mien communities (MacDonald, 1997). The Iu-Mien village allows families from other ethnic groups to reside near them, but not above them on the same mountain due to spiritual beliefs (Kandre, 1967; Moore-Howard, 1989). Where the village is or how it is constructed is less important than the location of the individual household (Lewis & Lewis, 1984). Due to spiritual beliefs, "no house is allowed to obstruct a clear line between any other house and the spirit shrines which are located above the village" (Kandre, 1967, p. 613).

Houses in Laos are made of wood and/or bamboo (T. Waters, personal communication, November 6, 2000) and are built on the ground. Roofs are constructed from grass, forming a thick layer (Gogol, 1996). The family home has two stoves, one for cooking the family's meals and one for cooking the pig's food. (The pig is spiritually significant and is discussed later in this chapter.) Homes are constructed with three doors. These include a "men's door" where guests enter, a "women's door" that leads to the kitchen, and a "big door" that is given this title because of its ceremonial importance. The "big door" is located directly across from the ancestral altar (Moore- Howard, 1989; Lewis & Lewis, 1984).

Houses may contain several bedrooms. Girls of marriageable age are given their own room to entertain suitors (Habarad, 1987b; Moore-Howard, 1989). This room is located next to the "women's door." Areas are set-aside for guests to stay and include a fireplace for their specific use.

Handcrafts-Needlework and Silversmithing
Embroidery

The Iu-Mien people are known for their very intricate embroidery. The clothing that is embroidered frequently consists of over 100 cross-stitch designs. The designs are described as continually evolving, and are a medium for demonstrating a person's creativity (Moore-Howard, 1989).

The designs are considered symbolic as well as decorative. The process of embroidery entails stitching on the back of the cloth, the side that will be on the inside of the clothing article. By completing the work in this fashion, the design is not apparent until the article is turned over, right side out, and revealed (Lewis & Lewis, 1984). Mothers elaborately embroider caps for their babies that include a red pompom on the top and with optional additional ones placed on the ears or edges of the cap. Clothing that contains embroidery includes sashes, aprons for weddings and New Year celebrations, pants, and bags for hunting or storing silver. In Laos, the material for clothing is obtained from trade with weavers.

Silver

Silver is a metal that is viewed as a sign of wealth. Silver coins were acquired from India during the British rule and French coins from Indochina. The Iu-Mien people make their own jewelry and are considered "highly skilled craftsmen " (Lewis & Lewis, 1984, p. 148). Many items that are made from silver include back chains of bells and coins, sickle shaped earrings, and specific wedding flowers for the brides' headdress (Kandre, 1967). Silver objects may be worn by an individual for life and may be viewed as a part of their body (Moore-Howard, 1989). Gold is not used in jewelry making; it is used solely for the purpose of dental work. Dentistry is considered somewhat of an "art" (T. Waters, personal communication, November 6, 2000).

Economy

The Iu-Mien people who farmed in the hills Laos were one of the wealthier groups in the area (Habarad, 1997b). The economy depended on hard work, interaction with those outside the community, and a collective ideology.

Opium

Opium has been a source of cash for the Iu-Mien people in Southeast Asia for many years. Kandre (1966) described this, stating at the time of his writing that it had been a cash crop "for at least the past fifty years" (p. 585). This would then mean that the cultivation of this crop was documented as early as 1916 in Thailand and Laos. Lewis & Lewis (1984) further discussed that the reasons for such an endeavor as opium is that it has a "high value for small volume; it can be grown at high elevation . . . it will not spoil . . . dealers come to the growers to make their purchases" (Lewis & Lewis, 1984, p. 18). A poppy field will produce for at least five to 10 years.

The French encouraged opium development during the colonial era and the development was continued by leftover French war veterans and renegades when the military withdrew in 1954 (McCoy, 1972). Opium has been officially an illegal crop in Southeast Asian since 1959 (Lewis & Lewis, 1984). However, it was encouraged by many, regardless of the law. Highland groups in Laos, including the Hmong and the Iu-Mien, were involved in the opium trade. Opium was also used as a source of medicine (T. Waters, personal communication, November 6, 2000).

The CIA was involved in Laos during the early 1960s in an effort to maintain the anti-Communist movement. When CIA monies were cut due to the Laotian government's refusal to follow U. S. demands concerning governmental leadership, the opium business grew. Fadiman (1997), in her book *The Spirit Catches You and You Fall Down*, provided a description of the opium trade that was supported by the CIA beginning in the mid-1960s:

> Realizing the best way to guarantee Hmong collaboration was to support their opium trade, the CIA used its Air American aircraft to pick up crude opium bricks in remote villages, and gave Vang Pao [the Hmong general] his own airline, Xieng Khouang Air Transport (nicknamed "Air Opium"), which flew opium from the secret Hmong military base at Long Tieng, in northern Laos, to markets in Vientiane. After it was refined, much of the Hmong opium crop ended up in South Vietnam, which it helped addict an estimated 30,000 American soldiers to heroin. A large portion subsidized the Armee Clandestine, which is one reason the war was such a bargain. (p. 130)

This intervention by the CIA is also well documented by McCoy (1972), who provided a detailed account of the Laotian government's view that "their only valuable export commodity is opium" (p. 250).

Although the Iu-Mien people were involved in the opium trade, few became opium addicts. Opium was considered "too valuable as a trade good to allow consumption . . . only ill or aged were allowed to use opium regularly" (Moore-Howard, 1989, p. 20). Kandre (1967) quoted a circular letter from Thailand and Laos that he related was most likely written in 1947:

Opium is not good. Some people become rich by trading with it, but others lost their wealth smoking it. Because of opium one often comes into opposition with the government, and the result is suffering. (The author of this letter neither smokes nor drinks.) (p. 608)

Other Agricultural Products

The Iu-Mien economy in Laos was also dependent on other agricultural products such as rice and corn. The Iu-Mien people practiced swidden (slash and burn) agriculture (Grove, 1976) on the hillsides. Each year, leaders of the households in the village would participate in informal negotiations to determine the distribution and preparation of fields (Kandre, 1967). The agricultural products were used for economic needs as well as the basic food needs of the community (T. Waters, personal communication, November 6, 2000).

Families typically raised pigs, which have religious significance. Some families also propagated other small animals. The men would hunt and fish, while women gathered plants to be used as medicines and food (MacDonald, 1997).

Currency

The Iu-Mien system of currency in Laos was trading and bartering. As stated previously, French Indochinese silver coins were greatly valued. Silver was the "ideal medium of exchange" (Moore-Howard, 1989, p. 15). Money, particularly silver, was seen as "the key to success . . . a bridge between the world of men . . . the world of spirits . . . " (Kandre, 1967, p. 597).

Employment in the United States

As discussed previously, Iu-Mien refugees were initially provided public assistance upon entering the United States. Previous job skills were not transferable in many areas. Thus, individuals from the Iu-Mien community tended to be placed in low-paying forms of employment. Saetern (1998) related that these included the work of custodians, gardeners, childcare workers, and aides in classrooms and health care programs. The children of refugees or those who immigrated during their early or teen years have found greater employment opportunity due to increase language and educational training.

Language and Education

Language

The Iu-Mien and the Hmong (another highland group) languages are linguistically distinct. The Iu-Mien language is a tonal system. Although the spoken language is more related to Hmong language than to other languages, it is quite different (Moore-Howard, 1989). The Iu-Mien language is monosyllabic with five tones that distinguish one word from another.

MacDonald (1997) noted that there are three separate languages that serve different meanings. These include a vernacular language for everyday communication, a Chinese form for formal uses such as the reading of circular letters, and Chinese for use with rituals. The Iu-Mien people are considered "the linguists of the mountains" (T. Waters, personal communication, November 6, 2000).

Education

The characters of the traditional Iu-Mien language are based in Chinese script. The skill in Chinese characters was apparent in the Iu-Mien people by the fourteenth century (MacDonald, 1997). More recently, some Iu-Mien individuals have adapted the Thai and Lao alphabet to write their language (Center for Applied Linguistics, 1981; Waters, 1990).

The primary written form for recording religious rituals, keeping family records, letters, and contracts was Chinese. Books have been written in Chinese that focus on myths (such as the origins of the Iu-Mien) and rituals (e.g. levels of bride price). There are collections of love songs and messages from leaders in the form of circular letters that were passed through areas where the Iu-Mien people lived (Kandre, 1967; MacDonald, 1997). MacDonald (1997) reported on a 1990 circular letter in the United States from an Iu-Mien Lao leader living in Thailand.

In Laos, only a few boys were taught to read and write by their fathers or Chinese teachers. Girls were excluded from the lessons (Smith & Tarallo, 1993). Chinn (2000) related that "it would be a waste [to educate girls] because girls would leave home and marry boys in some other family . . . women at the time did not get to make decisions as men" (p. 4).

Missionaries in the 1940s provided Western education to the Iu-Mien people. The Iu-Mien people who resided in northern Thailand were educated with a Romanized alphabet. This alphabet was used to record their everyday speech and was in script for reading of the Bible and health-related books.

After World War II, the Iu-Mien people became more involved with lowland villages. The trading with lowland groups increased the use of the Lao and Chinese languages. The education of the Iu-Mien people varied as it depended on where a person worked, and if he or she remained in her/his highland community or interacted with the lowlands. However, prior to 1975, the Iu-Mien people who resided in Laos' more remote areas were effectively excluded from what little formal education existed (Smith & Tarallo, 1993). Waters (personal communication, November 6, 2000) related that this was not unique to the Iu-Mien people as all rural residents were excluded due to poverty and discrimination. During the CIA involvement in Lao, sons of wealthy families who were involved in the war were educated in larger towns. American advisors provided English language and specialized training in an academy in Thailand for a few Iu-Mien individuals each year (MacDonald, 1997).

Currently, rough estimates of Iu-Mien college graduates in the United States reveal that 180 have earned bachelor's degrees, 20 have earned master's degrees, and several are in the process of obtaining doctorates (Chinn, 2000). In Yaangh's (2001) study of Iu-Mien high school graduates in the Sacramento City Unified School District, he noted that, of 30 graduates in the year 2000, 63% were female. He stated that this is significant data due to the comparison of education of females in Laos versus the United States. He related, "given the equal opportunity, women have exceeded men in the pursued (sic) of education" (p. 27).

In 1984, an Iu-Mien script developed by the Iu-Mien and an American linguist Dr. Herbert C. Purnell, was adopted in Portland, Oregon. Primers are now available in this script and literacy classes have been taught in the United States, China, and refugee camps in Thailand (MacDonald, 1997; Moore-Howard, 1989). Traditional stories have been recorded and published in English and Iu-Mien script, helping to preserve the culture of storytelling (Beard, Warrick, & Saefong, 1993; 1995). Yaangh (2001) related that some Iu-Mien leaders have suggested that less than 10% of the Iu-Mien in the United States are able to read and write in the script.

Effects of Imperialism

As a small minority, the Iu-Mien people have often been caught in the middle of battles. In Laos, the Iu-Mien people became threatened by fighting between French, lowland Lao, and highland factions as the French worked to colonize the region. In World War II, the Japanese invaded and occupied their settlements for use in staging operations against strongholds in southern China. From 1960-1975, the United States, without the knowledge of the American public, sponsored a war within Laos. It was termed by the United States military personnel, and then by the Iu-Mien and Hmong, as "The Secret War of the CIA." MacDonald (1997) stated that the Iu-Mien people in the United States designate 1962 "as the year which their traditional culture began to change as a result of their increased contact with Americans and the lowland Lao . . . [this was] the first time the Iu-Mien became refugees of the Indochinese War" (p. 88).

The CIA recruited the Iu-Mien and the Hmong as part of an irregular military force called by the Lao as the "Armee clandestine." The Iu-Mien in Laos were considered mercenaries by the CIA and were subsidized with rice and provided with shelter when they were forced to escape violence due to the war. Their job was to prevent North Vietnamese troops from bringing supplies through the region en route to South Vietnam.

When Laos fell in 1975 to the Communist regime, they expected to be helped by the CIA, but were in essence deserted by the CIA (MacDonald, 1997). Many of the Iu-Mien people worked to accommodate the new communist government. However, following persecution by the communists, the Iu-Mien people attempted to escape to refugee camps in Thailand. They traveled by foot through the jungle, crossing the Mekong River. Many were killed or died during their journey to the camps. Gogol (1996) related that approximately two-thirds of the Iu-Mien individuals residing in Laos were able to escape. Their goal was to rejoin their family in Thailand and escape persecution (T. Waters, personal communication, November 6, 2000). Resettlement to the United States came later.

In 1975, the first sets of refugees who were accepted for resettlement in the United States had to prove that they were directly part of the clandestine force or Royal Lao Army (Smith & Tarallo, 1993). This group has frequently been referred to in the literature as the "first wave" of refugees and the majority were Vietnamese (Harmon, 1995). They did not reside in refugee camps in Thailand or the Philippines, but instead stayed for a short time on military bases in the United States to gain English language skills and cultural orientation (Harmon, 1995).

Many refugees were prevented from entering the United States in the 1970s because of the requirements for documenting service to the United States. The "second wave" of refugees was primarily from Laos and Cambodia and consisted of ethnic minorities. These included the Hmong and Iu-Mien people who had resided in rural areas and experienced much hardship in their escape to refugee camps. Because of their remote, irregular status, the Iu-Mien people had a more difficult time establishing a U.S. connection.

Due to strong religious beliefs, the secret war and subsequent dislocations have had a profound effect on the Iu-Mien people, leaving them with "a deep sense of dislocation from their protective spirits" (Smith & Tarallo, 1993, p. 98). Smith and Tarallo (1993) recorded the fears of an Iu-Mien refugee in California in regard to the loss of rituals and customs in the United States.

70

Some older people worry here about the spirits and the religious ceremonies. If the older men pass away, nobody will know how to do it unless the young children learn how. First they have to learn to read and write in Chinese, and then they can learn to do the ceremonies . . . I don't see anybody learning embroidery . . . they probably won't know how to do it anymore. The older people worry . . . . the young people don't know how to dress. . . put the turban on . . . when they get married, probably that's the only time they will wear Mien clothes . . . but they'll always be Mien. Even with no religion, no ceremonies. (p. 103)

Summary

The experience of the refugees from Laos was not only of multiple cultural changes, but also of emotional trauma. The war in Southeast Asia was unpopular to many in the United States and was more complicated than the U. S. Administration led the public to believe. When the "secret war of the CIA" officially ended, it left thousands of Southeast Asians fearful of persecution. Thus began the flood of refugees from Laos into camps along the border of Thailand in 1975.

When Southeast Asian refugees arrived in the United States, they were scattered throughout the United States. For those who worked with the refugees, respect for the culture was paramount in addition to the understanding of the trauma and extreme cultural shock the refugees experienced. The individuals who possessed limited or no English language skills reported greater intergenerational conflict, greater dependency on others to negotiate American institutions, and felt less comfortable in the United States.

The Iu-Mien people of Laos have been described as experiencing isolation from the "outside" world (Chao, 1999). The "outside" world seems to mean European culture and some of the mechanisms of modern technology. Although the traditional Iu-Mien culture differs greatly from European culture, the Iu-Mien people in Laos maintained a very intricate and rich culture through a transnational existence. They maintained an oral language and recorded historical and religious material through the use of Chinese characters. This literacy was not acknowledged by the scholars and teachers, cited early in this chapter, who wrote of the Iu-Mien refugee experience outside and within the United States. Many of the researchers categorized the Iu-Mien people as "illiterate," seeming to imply that if the individual did not speak, read, and/or write in *English*, they were not literate.

Within the United States, the 1.5 generation (those born outside the United States, but who came to the United States prior to adolescence) who are published in literary journals and Web pages, describe the conflict with EuroAmerican of the Iu-Mien culture values and beliefs. There is a great need for the Iu-Mien perspective to be presented in an academic genre, to provide the credibility and access of information most often sought by academic scholars. Until there is greater information available to the public and academic institutions from the perspective of the Iu-Mien people, the presentation of the Iu-Mien culture will be "produced and [will] exists in an uneven exchange with various kinds of power . . . political power . . . power intellectual . . . power culture . . . [and] power moral" (Said, 1978, pp. 90-91). That is, the culture may not be viewed in its depth and resilience, but rather as simply a unique and unusual phenomenon from a Western perspective.

Habarad (1987b) related, "interplay is a large part of the interactive processes whereby peoples and their social organizations are transformed in contexts of change" (p. 7). The traditions from Laos are being transformed in the United States. The spiritual beliefs are central to the traditional Iu-Mien culture and while parts are being maintained, sources seem to indicate that mainstream EuroAmerican culture is being adopted by the 1.5 generation. Kelly, the female protagonist in *Kelly Loves Tony* (Nakasako, 1998), stated, "I want the American Dream . . . a big house, make a lot of money, be the perfect mom . . . I can't change the past, but I can change the future."

Chapter 4

Social Work Education: The Training Of Extension Agents?

To understand issues of cultural competency, it is important to also examine theories relating to the roles of social workers as "extension agents" of the dominant society. These include theories of education that apply to social work. Paulo Freire's analysis of social workers' role as instruments of oppression and their potential to be collaborative agents of change with the oppressed provides social worker with a powerful framework for examining cultural competency.

Sociological theories of ethnocentrism, assimilation, and cultural pluralism also relate well to social work education and practice. An examination of these will help to gain an understanding of the role of the educational institutions in the socialization of social workers.

Social Workers as Extension Agents

Paulo Freire, born in Brazil in 1921, was a lawyer who practiced social work as the director of the Department of Education and Culture of the Social Service in the State of Pernambuco (Collins, 1977). He later received a doctorate and became the director of the University of Recife's Cultural Extension Service where he developed a teaching method to increase literacy in Brazil (Collins, 1977). In 1964, over 16 million Brazilians 14 years and older did not read or write (Freire, 1998). For those adults who participated in his program, a large percentage learned to read and write in 45 days (Collins, 1977). Freire focused on the masses and their "right to participate in their liberation" (Collins, 1977, p. 69). His teaching technique was political in nature, viewing literacy as a means for the poor to recognize their oppression by the dominant social structure by developing critical consciousness.

Thus, the teachings of Paulo Freire (1998) seem very appropriate when evaluating the role of social workers in working with the oppressed, the non-dominant, in EuroAmerican society. Freire's perspective of social workers focused on their work as instruments of oppression. He stated:

> During the phase of the closed society, the people are *submerged* in reality. As that society breaks open, they *emerge.* No longer *mere spectators,* they uncross their arms, renounce expectancy, and demand intervention. No longer satisfied to watch, they want to participate. This participation disturbs the privileged elite, who band together in self-defense.
>
> At first, the elite react spontaneously. Later . . . they organize. They bring forth a group of "crisis theoreticians" (the new cultural climate is usually labelled (sic) a crisis); they create social assistance institutions and *armies of social workers*; [italics added] and—in the name of the supposedly threatened freedom—they repeal the participation of the people. (p. 14)

Social workers, in this light, are extension agents. They are technicians who work to "domesticate" the client to the world of the dominant culture, and in turn, extend the view of the dominant culture. From this perspective, the clients served by social workers are not challenged to think, critically reflect, and/or take their own action.

Freire (1985) stated that "the social worker, along with others, acts in a social structure . . . " (p. 38). Social workers who "mythicize reality," that is keep options for the client a secret and claim neutrality in the process, help to maintain the status quo. The social worker in this context favors "'normalization' of the 'established order,' which serves the power elite's interests" (Freire, 1985, p. 39).

Freire (1998) stated:

> the moment social workers define their work as *assistencialism* (term used in Latin American to describe policies of financial social "assistance" which attack symptoms, but not causes of social ills . . . overtones of paternalism . . . .) and yet say that it is educational, they commit a mistake which has fatal consequences . . . if a social worker (in the broadest sense) supposes that s/he is '*the* agent of change,' then it is with difficulty that s/he will see the obvious fact that, if the task is to be really education and liberating, those with whom s/he works cannot be the object of her actions. Rather, they too will be agents of change. If the social worker cannot perceive this, they will succeed only in the manipulating, steering and 'domesticating.' If on the other hand they recognize others, as well as themselves, as agents of change, they will cease to have the exclusive title of '*the* agent of change.' (p. 116).

In *Letters to Cristina* (1996), Freire provided a retrospection of his life and philosophies. In these writings, he addressed his view of social services and stated that he was not negating needed and indispensable assistance that was provided through social service programs. What he was against was ". . . the paternalistic mentality of the assistance programs, which anesthetized the political consciousness of those who receive assistance" (Freire, 1996, p. 98). Freire (1996) viewed the paternalism of those in power as manipulating the masses through this "ideological trap" (p. 98). Fritze (2000), who applied Freire's concepts to community work with women, mirrored Freire's voice. She stated,

> in welfare work as well as education, people can be oppressed by the thinking, language and behaviour (sic) of others. Community workers, teachers, social workers, etc. can perceive themselves as closer to the truth and reality than the people they are working with (students, clients). (p. 4)

Collins (2000) described Freire's view that social workers can be change agents who demythologize reality by reframing a client's view of reality as a problem to be posed. Thus, if the social worker participates in naming the oppression, the worker also raises his or her consciousness. The worker then questions the culture of silence by validating that there is a "world of deceit designed to increase their alienation and passivity…"(Freire, 1999, p. 120). That is, the social worker in this role is one of advocate, social organizer, and collaborator. For example, when a social worker evaluates an ethical dilemma, there must be a dialogue, problem posing, an assessment of the social structure, and involvement as an agent for change.

In *Sobre la Acción Cultural* (1970), Freire related that

> *El trabajador social que opta por el cambio no teme la libertad, no prescribe, no manipula; no huya a la communicación, por el contrario, la busca, más que la busca, la vive. Todo su esfuerzo de carácter humanista, se centra en el sentido de la desmitificación del mundo, de la desmitificación de la realidad. Ve en los hombres con quienes, jamás sobre quienes o contra quienes trabaja, personas y no cosas, sujetos y no objectos.* (pp. 128-9)

> The social worker who opts for change does not fear freedom, doesn't prescribe, nor manipulates; doesn't avoid communication, on the contrary, he/she looks for it, and more that looks for it, lives it. All of his effort, of humanist character is found in the feeling of demystification of the world, from the demystification of reality. He sees in men whom he never works over or against them, people and not things, subjects and not objects. (pp. 128-9)

Thus, the social worker may be utilized by the dominant culture as a socialization agent, a worker to "domesticate" the masses. But, the worker has the choice to view clients, patients, consumers (or any other term used to signify "the other") as subjects, to work together, collaboratively for social change.

The United States Government as an Extension Agent

The United States seemed unprepared for the mass exodus of individuals from Southeast Asia, and initial programming for the refugees was minimal. It was over a 15 to 20 year time span that programs became more innovative and addressed the *real* needs of the refugees. During the early years of refugee education, it seems that the teachers were a caricature of the extension agents as described by Paulo Freire (1998).

The extension agent, that is, the teacher who was the subject, transferred knowledge, depositing it into the minds of the refugees who were the passive objects. Education was for the purpose of domestication of the refugee into the ideal, middle class, American culture. Freire (1998) stated that the "fundamental task of the extension agent is 'to persuade the rural masses to accept our *propaganda.*' It is impossible to affirm that persuasion to accept *propaganda* is an educational activity" (p. 96). Thus, we may question if the attempt to replicate the American high school experience in the camps was propaganda or education.

The View of Ethnocentrism, Assimilation, and Cultural Pluralism

in Social Work Education

The question persists: Does the teaching of cultural competency in social work education, the content and manner in which material is taught, reflect themes of EuroAmerican assimilation and ethnocentrism or does it predominantly emphasize cultural pluralism? The subsequent discussion addresses the topics in the following order: (a) history of social work education, (b) social work literature, (c) social work faculty, (d) students' perceptions, and (e) field studies. Much has been written on models for teaching cultural diversity, oppression, and social justice in undergraduate and graduate social work programs. However, there appears to be much less research on the short-term and/or long-term effects of the models on actual social work practice.

The largest professional social work organization, the National Association of Social Workers (NASW) (2000), boasts a membership of 155, 000. As related previously, the NASW Code of Ethics (1997) views the acquisition of cultural competency as an ethical standard. Cultural competency entails social workers acquiring a basic understanding of the cultures in American society, maintaining sensitivity to these cultures, and understanding the factors that impact oppression in our society in regard to diversity (NASW, 1997).

The sole accrediting agency for social work education programs in the United States, the Council on Social Work Education (CSWE), was founded in 1952. The CSWE (2000) currently reports representing 142 graduate and 439 undergraduate programs. The CSWE (1999) mandates the teaching of cultural competency in their guidelines for baccalaureate programs. The 1999 guidelines state that the students' coursework needs to focus on understanding and respecting diverse populations. Additionally, the focus needs to include an understanding the influence of oppression to work towards the development of strategies for social change.

The History of Social Work Education

Social work's roots in the United States were planted primarily by middle class EuroAmerican women. Social work, previously termed as social welfare, has a long history that initially began as a focus on caring for those in need. It expanded to the development of programs designed to increase the well being of all members of the society, advocate for solutions to social problems, and work towards prevention (Trattner, 1974).

The majority of early social work ignored people of color, focusing on work with European immigrants (Potocky, 1997). An exception was the settlement house workers, who in the early 1900s worked for the establishment of the National Association for the Advancement of Colored People and the National Urban League (Potocky, 1997). Potocky (1997) described the primary model of social work in the 1870s-1950s as focusing on assimilation, viewing ethnic minorities as deviants. An "anti-racism" model was slightly less prevalent during the 1890s-1910s. This model focused on the reduction and prevention of ethnocentrism, prejudice, and "individual racism" (Potocky, 1997, p. 321).

Social work education has evolved from agency, on-the-job training in charitable organizations, to university education at the undergraduate and graduate level. The first official professional training program, provided for "charity workers" (Leighninger, 2000, p. 1), was at the New York Summer

School of Applied Philanthropy in 1898. The Columbia University School of Social Work became the first professional school. Over time, the schools that followed developed graduate programs within university settings. Austin (1997) reported that it was assumed that the primarily female student body would have already received a liberal arts degree. The students were trained by social workers who were practicing in the field.

In the 1930s, undergraduate programs were developed to meet agency staffing needs that resulted from the New Deal public welfare programs. In the 1960s, graduate social work programs grew dramatically. In the 1970s, baccalaureate social work programs were accredited by the Council on Social Work Education (CSWE) (Austin, 1997). The CSWE developed curriculum guidelines to address the needs of communities and individuals from nondominant groups and provided a distinctive focus on diversity (Leighninger, 2000).

Currently, statistics indicate that the majority of social work students continue to be women and that women of color are underrepresented (Morris, 1993). Morris (1993) related concern that "students and practitioners receive contradictory messages when they read about minority groups with which they are unfamiliar and at the time are cautioned not to generalize too broadly from myths and stereotypes" (p. 108-109).

The assumption in social work education is that if social work students understand the concepts of ethnocentrism and cultural pluralism, they can learn to tailor programs to meet the cultural needs of clients. However, Graham (1999) noted that there is an ethnocentric approach of social work in the United States that has developed from the perspective of an EuroAmerican focal point, viewing individuals as lacking skills. This ethnocentric frame of reference is exemplified by map projections that "reinforce historic patterns of world dominance" (Castex, 1993, p. 685). The community that is placed in the center of the map promotes a physical and/or psychological significance in regard to placement in the center or margins of a society.

Thus, "social work, consciously and unconsciously, has become an instrument of the Eurocentric worldview" (Graham, 1999, p. 105). Graham (1999) asserted that the profession of social work needs to "center each ethnic group in their own historical and cultural experiences . . . for a shift from the hegemony of ethnocentric paradigms of human knowledge to a culturally pluralistic one" (p. 105). Chau (1992) supported this view by stating that social work education needs to teach "how ethnocentric attitudes and cognitions can perpetuate fallacious and prejudicial interactions and interventions on the part of practitioners" (p. 4). Mason, Benjamin, and Lewis (1996) related a " . . . hindrance to promoting cultural pluralism in the current education and training of professionals" (p.172).

Some scholars who evaluate the depth of understanding of cultural competency that social work graduates demonstrate question the worker's ability in regard to their actual work with clients from diverse cultural backgrounds (Yuen & Pardeck, 1998). Potocky (1997) assessed the multicultural approach of social work and concluded that "social workers [need] to directly address ethnocentrism, assimilationism, prejudice and racism in their work with clients" (p. 320). To combat ethnocentrism, the social work profession has adopted an antidiscriminatory perspective. The focus is on

> limiting the damage within social work practice that preaches the worth of every individual yet supports institutional and cultural racism at every level . . . [to] attempt(s) to combat racism in the system and within the professional subjective judgment of social workers . . . [to create a] reactive stance against racism and oppression. (Graham, 1999, p. 104)

Taylor-Brown, Garcia, and Kingson (2001) provided the perspective that in the endeavor to achieve cultural competency, "cultural chauvinism" (p. 185) may emerge. This happens when the emphasis is on having only members of the same ethnic or cultural group provide services for that specific group, rather than provided "individualized social services within a culturally appropriate context" (Taylor-Brown, Garcia, & Kingson, 2001, p. 185).

Social Work Literature

McMahon and Allen-Meares (1992) used a content analysis of major articles published in refereed social work journals between 1980-1989 to examine the field's attention to issues of diversity. Out of 1,965 articles, McMahon and Allen-Meares (1992) found that 117 "proposed some form of social work intervention with minorities" (p. 534), " . . . to adjust to their situation" (p. 536). The group targeted in the majority of articles was African Americans. Ninety-one articles focused on individual intervention to assist social workers in increasing their cultural awareness by expanding knowledge and/or skills. and 26 recommended policy change within institutions.

The lack of articles that focus on minorities suggested that "minorities are only a marginal concern for social work" (McMahon & Allen-Meares, 1992, p. 537). The authors stated that the "literature conveys the impression of a noncritical, inward-looking, even narcissistic, professional literature . . . [that] virtually ignores the societal context of the client . . . [implying] that minorities can only be assisted one by one" (McMahon & Allen-Meares, 1992, p. 536). The authors further stated that the literature is based on the ideology of assimilation, devaluing minorities " . . . by urging or expecting minority clients to accept and assimilate the social and family values of the majority society" (McMahon & Allen-Meares, 1992, p. 537).

Social work practice focuses on cultural sensitivity, but McMahon and Allen-Meares (1992) related that "if [the] literature reflects practice, one could conclude that social workers are not practicing what they advocate"(p. 537). They felt that "the literature portrays the social work profession as naive and superficial in its antiracist practice . . . [using a] color blind" (McMahon & Allen-Meares, 1992, p. 537) approach. That is, if a social worker is simply culturally sensitive, racism will be removed from the client. Their assessment of this view "reveals a racist attitude in some of the surveyed literature because it views minorities' oppression as normal and natural" (McMahon & Allen-Meares, 1992, p. 537). To be antiracist, the authors noted that there must be "transformative action to remove the conditions that oppress people" (McMahon & Allen-Meares, 1992, p. 537) by increasing social activism for justice and racial equality. This literature review did not cover the most recent decade, thus the following study is of interest.

Akerlund and Cheung (2000) used a keyword database search through Social Work Abstracts, PsychInfo, and Sociofile to perform a content analysis of articles written on minority gay and lesbian issues during 1989 to 1998. They found and reviewed 22 articles, noting that the most recent articles from 1998 may not have been included yet through this type of search. In this study, the researchers looked for common themes and concepts, categorizing the ethnic groups of African American, Asian American, and Latino.

Akerlund and Cheung (2000) reported that the literature seems to focus on deficits, such as barriers and negative experiences of gay and lesbian members of the ethnic groups. Due to this focus, the researchers stated that stereotypes and negative views may be reinforced regardless of the gender or age group. This supports the concern noted earlier that stereotypes are replicated in social work literature.

Akerlund and Cheung (2000) indicated that the articles seemed to focus little on strengths, commitments to end oppression, or a view of the "nonstatic nature of the search for identity" (p. 290). They stated a need to "focus on the analysis of strengths . . . [rather than] to be heavily focused on cultural stereotypes . . . " (p. 291). One weakness of this study, noted by the researchers, was the subjectivity of the content analysis and the categorizing of areas and themes.

Faculty

Singleton (1994) conducted in-depth interviews with 11 faculty from four urban East Coast schools of social work with BSW and MSW programs. Three of the universities had primarily white faculty and student body and one was termed "a predominately black university" (p. 7). The faculty was evaluated in regard to their personal comfort in teaching about oppression. Singleton (1994) found that the comfort level of faculty impacts the "repertoire of values, knowledge and skills transmitted to students" (p. 6).

Singleton evaluated transcripts from open-ended interviews, observing patterns in regard to life experiences, thought patterns, and behaviors. The faculty, when asked to define oppression yielded "virtually no discussion of homophobia, discrimination against the handicapped, the aged, anti-Semitism . . . " (p. 7). Some faculty seemed the most comfortable avoiding all together the word "oppression" and instead used the word "diversity." An EuroAmerican instructor stated "'we don't use the word oppression in the curriculum; we talk about dealing with people who are different'" (p. 8). This seemed to be an ethnocentric viewpoint. Singleton related, "avoidance of the term 'oppression' often derived from the notion that oppression distinctly implies the existence of oppressors" (p. 8).

Singleton's study presented a continuum; some faculty avoided all content that appeared to indicate oppression while others were quite blatant in focusing on oppression. This was due to a faculty member's "lack of direct experience of being oppressed [which] can be an important part of the rationale not to teach oppression content" (Singleton, 1994, p. 9). Some EuroAmerican faculty felt they did not have expertise in the area, while another, who worked at the predominately African American university, felt the need to " 'double and triple' his own studies and to achieve a high level of oppression content" (Singleton, 1994, p. 10). African American teachers at white universities reported great motivation to share their experiences. The setting of the university appeared to impact the motivation to gain more comfort in the topic.

Many students were reported to resist and complain to faculty about feeling uncomfortable in the classes. However, other participants in the study reported students responding positively, learning a new perspective. The faculty, who were employed by EuroAmerican institutions, seemed to share more negative experiences with the students and their colleagues stating, "'the white faculty are going around making denials about the existence of racism . . . [are] angry, lashing out and accusing people of being anti-white'" (Singleton, 1994, p. 15).

Another study that complemented Singleton's (1994) was a survey of 16 social work professors completed by Garcia and Van Soest (1999). They applied critical incident methodology to identify critical events in teaching about oppression. This is a technique that is used to assist emergency service workers evaluate the subjective and objective outcomes of an incident, including client changes. Garcia and Van Soest (1999) viewed this method useful to prepare faculty for the strong emotions that the topic of oppression might elicit from students. They noted the "faculty often find themselves struggling with how to transform strained classroom interaction into a 'teachable moment' that uses the interaction as a focus of cognitive and emotional learning" (p. 150).

The faculty in this study were 63% female and EuroAmerican. Nineteen percent were African American and 19% were Latino. The make-up of students in the classes ranges from 40% to 80% EuroAmerican. A course on diversity was required by 88% of the programs.

Strong emotions from students concerning the topics of gay and lesbian parenting, bilingualism, and racism triggered what the authors viewed as critical events. Faculty reported that some of the reactions were a result of students' racism or resistance. Half the faculty reported positive outcomes, defined by increases in student respect, open and honest classroom communication, and personal growth. Six of the events reported had negative outcome when the faculty was unable to reframe the experience into a teachable moment. Faculty reported difficulty in these areas due to lack of skills for effectively addressing the situation, being surprised by an outburst, and having their own feelings impede the learning process.

The themes from the research indicated that help with summarizing student learning, facilitating students' willingness to stay with the sensitive topic, and using oneself in the teaching such as modeling acceptance and appropriate use of anger, lead to the least traumatic experience for the teachers as well as the students. In general, there were many reported incidents of challenges in teaching about diversity. Garcia and Van Soest (1999) related a need to "legitimize learning about emotions . . . and critical thinking in order to prepare students for some of the struggles they will encounter as practitioners dealing with diversity issues" (p. 163).

Both studies on social work faculty presented a small sample. There appears to be difficulty in evaluating whether the themes reported could be generalized to other university settings in different regions of the country and with a different mix of ethnic groups. Another limitation was that the individuals in this study were primarily EuroAmerican and female.

Student Perceptions

Bronstein and Gibson (1998) conducted a survey of 57 full-time students in a graduate social work program. All participants were enrolled in a required second of three sequenced courses termed "Methods of Direct Practice" (p. 160). A self-administered survey, given the third week of class, contained a combination of open and closed ended questions. These included the students' level of satisfaction as to the course content on oppression, their recommendations for change, and perceptions as to the commitment the instructor seemed to present on the issue of oppression.

The respondents consisted of 89% female; 67% were "White Non-Hispanic" (p. 162). Bronstein and Gibson (1998) noted the timing of the survey stating, " seventy percent . . . indicated that their current Practice course had not yet included content on oppression . . . not completely surprising given that it was only the third week of the semester" (p. 161). This seemed to be a weakness of the study.

Overall, the data from the study seemed to indicate that if the students perceive their teacher as a member of an oppressed population, students were more likely to self-evaluate their own views. The students related that this person was "better able to teach content on oppression" (p. 165) through personal stories. The study also found that social work content contains material on oppression, but that the students "lack the ability to link group-specific knowledge to the overall influence of oppression on the lives of people" (Bronstein & Gibson, 1998, p. 165). Ethnocentrism seemed alive, though perhaps subtle, as exemplified in a statement by a Non-Hispanic White female, "I want to understand where the system went wrong and why *they* are not motivated to raise themselves and not want welfare and free money" (p. 163). Two "White Hispanic" (p. 163) females related wanting to know about "*their* [others'] history...[how] *they* become oppressed" (authors added the italics) (p. 163). Bronstein and Gibson (1998) noted that the students in their study "perceive[d] oppression as something that occurs outside of their own personal experience" (p. 163).

In another study, Van Soest (1994) completed a two-phase exploratory field study to gain an understanding of Master's of Social Work students' view on a new course that focused on diversity and oppression. Ninety-seven students participated in the total study. The first phase consisted of a content analysis of 30 student journals in one of three sections of the course. Seventy percent of the participants were EuroAmerican and 80% were female. In the second phase, a questionnaire was administered to all three sections of the course. It asked the student to describe what they learned about oppression, how it related to them personally, and how interaction with their peers and professor affected their learning in regard to multiculturalism.

The results of both phases of the study indicated that it is important for students to share their own experiences of oppression with their peers. Van Soest (1994) stated that "broadness or narrowness of one's moral boundaries is influenced by attitudes which are shaped by prevailing cultural norms" (p. 24). The EuroAmerican students appeared to become more aware and empathic of non-EuroAmericans expanding their "moral boundaries . . . [changing their] perceptions of themselves and their identity as benefactor, perpetrator or victim of oppression . . . " (p. 25-26).

Yuen and Pardeck (1998) evaluated 153 students in their junior year in an undergraduate social work program who had completed a course on human diversity. They used a cross-sectional pre/post survey that includes 24 items with non-randomized comparison groups over a three-year period. Comparison groups were advanced and beginning students.

There were several weaknesses of the study including that only 48 students completed both the pre- and post-test survey. One hundred and sixteen students completed the pre-survey and 85 completed the post survey. The researchers did not provide data on ethnic breakdown of participants.

Yuen and Pardeck (1998) did note that "systematic assessment of the outcome of such inclusion in social work education however are insufficient . . . current study provides basic indications of the positive effect" (p. 259) course on human diversity. The results from those completing the survey immediately after the course, compared with those of more advanced social work students, indicated that there was a positive impact on attitudes towards appreciation of diversity that lasted over time within the social work program.

Field Work

Scholars who evaluate the depth of understanding of cultural competency that social work graduates demonstrate have questioned the graduates' ability in regard to their actual work with clients from diverse cultural backgrounds (Yuen & Pardeck, 1998). Mason, Benjamin, and Lewis (1996) related a " . . . hindrance to promoting cultured pluralism in the current education and training of professionals . . . " (p.172). Several studies have been conducted to assess whether what is taught in school translates to actual practice.

Rittner, Nakanishi, Nackerud, and Hammonds (1999) conducted a nationwide telephone survey of 104 agency-based MSW social workers during the 1995-96 academic school year. They employed a convenience sample using a snowball technique, gaining access through social work groups and word of mouth. They utilized a "semi-structured questionnaire" (p. 423).

The goal of the research was to "determine if current content in MSW curricula helps social workers conduct assessments of diversity factors and plan interventions with attention to culturally competent practice in their work with small groups" (p. 423). The researchers evaluated the participants' exposure to diversity content in their social work program, their own sociocultural identity, the types of diversity groups they worked with, and the strategies of intervention. Rittner, Nakanishi, Nackerud, and Hammonds (1999) related that the participants reported a great deal of coursework in diversity, but experienced difficulty applying the material in their professional settings. The researchers stated that the participants were

> most likely to evaluate diversity by the most overt or visual categories; culture, immigration status, and race . . . [but] may not recognize the dynamics introduced by gender differences in groups . . . apply diversity content in a very limited way . . . use only a few interventions to address diversity in their groups . . . . (p. 419)

They concluded that

> . . . MSW-educated social workers enter practice inadequately prepared by curricular diversity content to address certain interactions among members of small groups . . . [they] lack of complexity in their characterizations of diversity . . . [and the authors] raise concerns about how MSW-educated social workers understand diversity. (p. 430)

Several weaknesses in this study seemed apparent. The researchers asked the participants to describe themselves, but the researchers did not tell the race, gender, sexual orientation, or cultural characteristics of the participants in the discussion of the study. Rittner, Nakanishi, Nackerud, and Hammonds (1999) related that in further studies, they would need a more systematic sampling strategy.

The Teaching Of Cultural Competency In Social Work Education

The social work literature addresses existing models used to teach cultural competency in undergraduate social work education. There is continual discussion as to the most effective fashion of addressing cultural competency. However, the literature lacks information from non-dominant groups regarding their experience with social workers. Thus, these experiences do not inform the models for teaching cultural competency. The importance of understanding an individual's culture is paramount in the practice of social work (Midgette & Meggert, 1991; Tasker, 1999; Van Voorhis, 1998). Current research describes many different methods for providing students the opportunity to learn about diverse cultures.

Teaching Theoretical Views of Oppression

Van Voorhis (1998) provided a teaching framework to prepare students for assessing "the impact of institutionalized oppression on their client" (p. 131), focusing on a theoretical base of oppression. Midgette and Meggert (1991) reported that counselors need to have knowledge of oppression in this country. Gutierrez, Fredricksen, and Soifer's (1999) survey of social work faculty revealed that faculty were "more supportive of content on [ethnic] groups than on oppression" (p. 417), leading the researchers to question the knowledge and value base of the faculty in this area. They suggested that the Council on Social Work Education (CSWE) curriculum policy statement may not be followed in regard to social justice and oppression.

Pinderhughes (1997) related the need for cultural competency in the field of child welfare. In the training of social workers, she stated that the individual needs to gain knowledge of "the dynamic of difference and power and how they operate in human functioning" (p. 20) and then, be able to apply this to the intervention process. Through this awareness, a worker would then be prepared to gain the skills of flexible thinking and behavior, awareness of one's stereotypes and "false beliefs" (p. 20), and gain comfort in working with those outside his or her familiar cultural context.

Chau (1990) related a need for providing a model that entails an ethnocultural content. In his course description, students first are taught terminology, key concepts "for differentiating ethnic clients or understanding them in terms of degree of cultural congruence, cultural resources available, problem-solving pattern[s] . . . variations in perception of needs, problem definition and solution" (p. 128). Following this, students participate in group activities with a focus on developing the "ability to distinguish their own world view from the world view of others" (p. 129).

The increased computer literacy of students has lead to the use of web-based course work. Van Soest (2000) utilized a course website for students to share reflections on material relating to cultural diversity. Outcomes indicated that when the web activity paralleled speakers or films in the class, use of this format increased, providing an opportunity for self-reflection and peer dialogue.

The debate as to the correct terminology and use of knowledge within the field of social work is lively. Atherton and Bolland (1997) suggested that social workers need to concentrate on understanding cultural diversity as well as working with the oppressed. They related that the debate on terminology "obscures and trivializes their [the oppressed] position" (p. 150).

Self-Reflection in the Classroom

In order to effectively explore the areas of cultural sensitivity and competency, the literature indicates the need to create a course that begins with honest self-reflection in a safe, supportive classroom environment. Self-reflection is a technique for students to become aware of their own cultural histories, values, biases, and beliefs. Wolfson (1992) described the need to develop ground rules within classrooms that include openly addressing stereotypes while building a community within the classroom to facilitate open discussions of difficult subjects. When the medium of teaching is through distance learning (satellite classrooms), cultural competency can be taught using creative techniques to promote confidentiality, open expression, trust, and, instructor-student exchange (Ancis, 1998).

Weaver (1999) noted that much of what is written about cultural competency is theoretical and that students need to assess their own views in order to gain respect and nonjudgmental attitudes towards varying cultures. In addition to evaluation of one's own attitudes, it is important to have an understanding of one's knowledge of "cross-cultural strengths and weakness" (Mason, 1995, p. 3). Assessment instruments are helpful for students to develop insight into their own value and knowledge base (Mason, 1995; Randall-David, 1994). In one study, students were provided pre- and post-test interviews to assess their perceptions of their self-identity (Garcia & Van Soest, 1997). The researchers noted an increase in cultural and self-awareness following a semester of self-analysis and sharing of personal stories within the classroom.

Chau (1990) utilized an "Ethnic Self Profiling" (p. 128) exercise that entails the development of word lists describing cultural diversities. Students rated the words as to their comfort level and view of the words. In groups, common themes were discussed and students were reported to develop awareness of their own and others' attitudes. Higher levels of self-awareness "provides a basis for appreciation of both similarities (culture-general) and differences (culture-specific) and world views" (Chau, 1990, p. 129) and the impact on social work practice and social policy.

Observation and Activities in the Classroom

Kieffer and Leach (1997) evaluated 91 graduate students in counseling psychology who were asked to analyze video-taped vignettes in regard to the cultural competency of counselors. The videos provided cultural variation of counselors and clients. Through class discussions, the students gained awareness of cultural issues and dynamics exhibited within the vignettes. Kieffer and Leach

(1997) recommended further research in this area to evaluate all the variables that may impact the students' perceptions.

Holland and Kilpatrick (1993) used fictional short stories to increase student awareness of cultural issues. The instructor chose the first set of stories that mirrored the students' backgrounds, followed by stories depicting other cultural groups. The class as a whole discusses the themes in the stories, strengths of the characters, cultural stereotypes and the influences on the character's life, modes of interpretation, and analysis in regard to social work practice. The goal of this type of activity was to change student perceptions of cultural issues by increasing self-awareness and understanding of one's own culture as well as others'. The activity provided a "bridge across differences . . . offer[ing] creative and empowering approaches to strengthening education for professional practice in a multicultural world" (p. 308).

Pierce and Taitano (1999) utilized "gaming simulations . . . to increase motivation and interest . . . broaden awareness of options . . . [and] probable consequences of particular policies or event . . . skill development in areas of critical thinking and analysis . . . " (p. 111) in regard to the teaching of oppression and techniques for social change. Their focus was on working with individuals who are gay or lesbian. The games were described as being easy to learn and play, but challenging enough to elicit critical analysis of real-life events. The authors developed two games; one simulated various contexts of homophobia and institutionalized heterosexism and the factors of oppression. The second focused on increasing sensitivity to the "oppressive continuum of hatred and violence" (p. 117).

In a similar light, Morris provided (1993) five themes (personal is political, interacting oppressions, importance of unique issues, stereotypes and myths, and power) as mediums for discussing cases that address issues of feminism and racism. Morris (1993) related that multiple sources, including research, popular fiction and films, students' own experiences and those of clients were used for case examples. The students participated in several activities designed to view the cases in relation to the themes. These include applying the themes to different coping techniques used in the cases, discussing in a group or writing individually about personal experiences, participating in role plays, debating controversial issues depicted in the cases, interviewing women of color, and playing games that dramatize the distribution of power. The integration of the themes and cases

> facilitate[d] the identification of students with those who are different from them in gender, race, experience, and enable all students to explore conflicting loyalties and values...[and facilitated] the involvement of the student on the personal as well as the intellectual level. (Morris, 1993, p. 108)

Cultural Sharing

Van Voorhis (1998) encouraged students to have their clients [in their internships] share their personal cultural story, and to read autobiographies, biographies, and fiction to find examples of their own and their clients' experiences. The University of Washington School of Social Work developed a cultural diversity course that included the use of intergroup dialogues, that is, face-to-face interactions with students from varying groups. Personal experiences were shared to increase knowledge not only of culture, but of oppression (Nagda, Spearmon, Holley, Harding, Balassone, Moise-Swanson, & de Mello, 1999).

Yuen and Pardeck (1998) required students in their human diversity course to participate in community activity or spend a day with an individual who would challenge the student's stereotypes and/or increase his or her knowledge about a cultural group. The students described this interactive process in positive terms. The result of a pre- and post-survey revealed increased awareness of the multiple issues facing non-dominant groups in the United States, and the role of the social worker as a change agent. The students "were 'forced' to deal with human diversity on a reality level; it was no longer an intellectual exercise in the classroom" (p. 252).

94

Cultural Immersion

Poole (1998) discussed the need to become culturally competent by immersing oneself in a culture. He facilitated two weeks of cultural immersion in Mexico to gain "knowledge of the varied elements within the larger cultural matrix of society . . . " (p. 164). Students lived with Mexican families and participated in a Spanish course. They visited social service agencies and cultural sites while residing in either rural or urban areas. Poole related, "there are good and bad traits in every culture. I want to encourage my students to lean towards tolerance but not accept or value cultural traits that harm or oppress people" (p. 166).

Another immersion program that focuses on the development of cross-cultural practice was described by Krajewski-Jaime, Brown, Ziefert, and Kaufman (1996). Junior level social work students participated in a seven week field placement at a hospital in Mexico City. A prerequisite to this experience was at least two years of high school Spanish or one year of college Spanish. The students resided with families, attended interdisciplinary seminars, and worked in the hospital with patients and their families providing direct service. The experience was described as a necessity for one to "never again possibly to take for granted that one's own way is the way of the universe" (p. 27). The authors discussed the movement of the students across a continuum from denial to an integration of cultural differences.

Summary

The literature seems to relate unequivocally that social work education within many different universities attempts to expose students to cultural pluralism. There appears to be some focus on teaching cultural pluralism/multiculturalism that encompasses the effects of oppression. Data indicated that faculty and students alike experience emotional reactions to the material that may cause to resistance to facilitate greater learning. The ethnic background of the faculty member may influence the student's perception of the credibility of the faculty in teaching about oppression and cultural pluralism.

Although the social work values (NASW, 1997) and the mandates from the Council on Social Work Education (1999) direct the teaching of cultural competency, it is uncertain if these attitudes and skills for working with diverse groups transfer to the field. The lack of studies and various weaknesses, especially the size of the samples and methodology, indicates a need for greater research in this area. Attitudes are very difficult to assess due to their subjective nature.

It seems necessary to evaluate these issues more fully from a non-EuroAmerican perspective in light of the majority of participants in the studies were EuroAmerican. Those who were non-EuroAmerican seemed the most vocal in expressing the need to evaluate carefully the educational practices for subtle, but pervasive, indicators of assimilationist and ethnocentric thought processes. It seems from the few studies that have been completed, that, as noted by McMahon and Allen-Meares (1992), social work is somewhat naïve in respect to the teaching of cultural competency.

The literature indicates that there are varying methods for teaching cultural competency ranging from simulations to direct interaction with members of varying cultural groups. In the attempts to teach cultural competency, students are encouraged to practice introspection, evaluating and confronting personal and societal stereotypes and attitudes. The literature does not reveal any studies or methods that directly address individuals from oppressed groups' experiences with social workers who demonstrated cultural competency or exhibited weakness in this area. Social Workers need to be continually educated as to the implication of the potential to become extension agents. The academic and practice community would benefit from further critical examination of cultural pluralism in order to live up to the National Association of Social Work Code of Ethics that emphasizes dignity, worth, and self-determination of clients (NASW, 1997).

Chapter 5

Participatory Research: Social Work Values Exemplified

This study was qualitative in nature, using participatory research as the single approach. The participants in the study were Iu-Mien social service workers employed in social service settings. The study focused on their perceptions of interactions with non-Iu-Mien social service workers and/or social workers, evaluating areas where the workers demonstrated cultural competency and/or seemed to lack cultural competency.

Participatory Research

Participatory research was most appropriate for the study due to the nature of the research questions and unique experiences of each participant. The theory behind qualitative research is that the researcher focuses on the "study of real-world situations . . . [in a] non-manipulative, unobtrusive, and non-controlling" fashion (Patton, 1990, p. 41). The volunteers, termed "participants," provide their own unique perspectives with their words directly quoted to exemplify their viewpoints, experiences, and ideas for change (Bogdan & Biklen, 1998; Patton, 1990).

Participatory research differs from traditional research, which views the subjects of the research as objects and seeks observable, objective facts (Kieffer, 1981; Maguire, 1997; Reason, 1994). Park (1993) stated that, "in participatory research, everybody connected with the project is informed of the intent and the logic of the questions, and is in a position to share knowledge with others" (p. 13). Participatory research is a "systematic approach to personal and social transformation"(Maguire, 1997, p. 3) that focuses on " . . . inclusion of its subjects as active partners throughout the research . . . in preliminary research design, in interactive generation of data, and in dialogic interpretation of the data as it is generated" (Kieffer, 1981, p. 3).

Participatory research and feminist research are considered by Joyappa and Martin (1996) as "empower-oriented approaches" (p. 2) that work to involve the participant(s) in sharing the control of the research process while affirming their subjective perspective as valid and "capable of generating knowledge" (p. 3). The researcher listens "to voices previously unheard . . . [and works to] amplify and disseminate the reflections of the people" (Ada & Beutel, 1993, p. 3). Thus, in comparing participatory research to traditional research, Kieffer (1981) related:

> If powerlessness is defined as the inability to co-constitute the events of one's everyday life-world, or the self-acceptance of the status of "object-hood," then the more traditional approaches to research reinforce this structure of oppression. (p. 15)

The term "participatory research" was first used in Tanzania in the early 1970s by individuals who were involved in the restructuring of the government. It was seen as a way to resist "colonial or neocolonial research practices" by those who were dominated (Hall, 1993, p. xv). This research method has strong roots in the work of Paulo Freire and focuses on liberation from oppression and from powerlessness, with the oppressed becoming an author of his/her own world. The participant is transformed from an object to a subject. As Freire (1999) stated, "to exist, humanly, is to *name* the world, to change it . . . human beings are not built in silence, but in word, in work, in action-reflection" (p. 69). Through naming the world comes liberation, the process of conscientization that leads to critical reflection (Freire, 1999). It is assumed in participatory research that "all human beings have the capacity to know" (Ada & Beutel, 1993, p. 3). Conscientization is a "human reflective action which expresses the knowing process whereby oppressed individuals and classes become subjects " (Collins, 2000, p. 221). One critically evaluates his or her perception of reality through exchanges with others, in effect, confronting the world, which in turn, leads to action for social change (Elias, 1994).

The Role of the Researcher

In participatory research, the researcher's role is not to judge or attempt to change the participant. Rather, the relationship between the researcher and participant is collaborative; they are co-researchers who will learn together through critical reflection. Critical reflection is considered a necessity in order "to bring about knowledge that will, later on, be the basis for action. The initial dialogic reflection is in itself the beginning of the emancipatory act" (Ada & Beutel, 1993, p. 28). In this process, the researcher is respectful of the cultural norms and values of the participant and the power in the relationship is shared, as a partnership. The researcher is an active member in the conversation with the participant, thus it is truly a dialogue with mutual exchange. In this context, both the researcher and participant are "learners and teachers of one another" (Ada & Beutel, 1993, p. 9). This active involvement leads to "a greater degree of both honesty about and control over the inevitability of subjective bias [and] prior assumptions" (Kieffer, 1981, p. 13).

Dialogue as the Medium for Knowledge

The premise behind participatory research that "the correct method lies in dialogue" (Freire, 1999, p. 49) lends itself to an inductive format. Themes emerge from open-ended questions developed to guide the dialogue in regard to individual experiences, specific to that participant. Concentration and practice is needed to learn the art of dialogue (Ada & Beutel, 1993). Debbink and Ornelas (1997) related the need for dialogue "to discover the intimacy of the subject . . .

intimacy is a type of soup made with honesty, sincerity, deepness, . . . it nourishes you . . . by knowledge . . . it is an act of creation and re-creation" (p. 19). Smith, Willms, and Johnson (1997) stated:

> The recovery of personal and social histories, reexamination of realities, and regaining of power through deliberate actions leads to the production of knowledge that can nurture, empower, and liberate persons and groups to achieve a more humane and equitable world. (p. 8)

The participatory approach "stresses the importance of human subjectivity and consciousness in knowledge creation" (Maguire, 1997, p. 19).

Participatory research is "not one-sided and antagonistic"(Patton, 1990, p. 345), rather, it "aims to develop critical consciousness to improve the lives of those involved in the research process, and to transform fundamental societal structures and relationships" (Maguire, 1997, p. 3). Kieffer (1981) related that participatory research "illuminate[s] the explicitly positive phenomenon of the empowerment of individuals . . . " (p.6). If the research views the participant as self-determining, then

> . . . what they do and what they experience as part of the research must be to some significant degree determined by them . . . [then] all those involved in the research are both co-researchers . . . generating ideas, designing and managing the project, and drawing conclusions from the experience, . . . and *also* co-subjects, participating in the activity being researched. (Reason, 1994, p. 326)

For the researcher, this approach requires introspection to gain an awareness of one's own values and experiences and how they impact the research process. The researcher is not a passive evaluator who is detached from the process in the attempt to provide an "objective" analysis.

Research and the Strengths Perspective

Participatory research exemplifies the strengths perspective that guides current social work practice. Altpeter, Schopler, Maeda, and Pennell (1999) related that participatory research "combines social work practice and research and that social work practitioners, because of their values and practice skills, can readily become equipped to undertake this research methodology" (p. 32). Hick (1997) reiterated that participatory research is appropriate for social workers because both the methodology and the researcher

> locates social problems in social structures, social relations and dominant ideology or knowledge, rather than in the individual or family . . . containing the distinctive viewpoint of dual transformation of control over the means of material production and over the means of knowledge production and the power to determine what is valid or useful knowledge. (p. 75)

Thus, as Park (1989) stated, "participatory research is a means of putting research capabilities in the hands of the deprived and disenfranchised people so that they can transform their lives for themselves . . . transform it as active participants" (p. 1).

The strengths perspective in social work views the assets and abilities of an individual versus deficits and "recognizes the importance of empowerment, resilience, healing, and wholeness in working with people" (Johnson & Yanca, 2001, p. 13). The social worker and the client work collaboratively with the philosophy that the client's strengths have "allowed them to survive and perhaps thrive in the face of adversity . . . " (Johnson & Yanca, 2001, p. 63). This is a mirror of the fundamentals of participatory research which establish

> the participant as subject of his/her own history and encourages shared control of the generation of knowledge. Understanding is jointly constructed in the process of research, rather than imposed as an alienated product. (Kieffer, 1981, p. 16)

Freire (1999) stated, "human beings are not built in silence, but in word, in work, in action-reflection . . . praxis . . . to transform the world . . . the right of everyone" (p. 69).

The Development of the Research Process

The history of the Iu-Mien people and their experiences in the United States provided a lens through which I examined the theory and practice in social work education. In the development of the research process, I invited social service workers from the Northern California Iu-Mien communities in Redding and Sacramento to participate in this study. In response to the relatively large concentration of Iu-Mien families in these communities, specific social service programs that targeted Iu-Mien community members are prevalent. These social services are provided through the schools, the mental health, and/or the public health care system.

An Overview of the Participants

The participants in this study were from the Iu-Mien community who were currently employed in social service settings in the role of social service worker or social worker. Five of the participants had not received a degree in social work, but were employed under the title of social service worker, human service worker, or similar connotation, supported by a job description that encompasses work in the helping profession.

I recruited the participants through community leaders, letters of request to social service agencies, and through referrals from other social service workers. Nonprobability sampling methods were used in this study; participants were selected in a non-random fashion. In order to secure participants who might not have been initially identified, a snowballing sampling or chain referral was initially implemented. This study was an excellent example of snowball sampling as many of the participants volunteered names and contacted potential participants for this researcher.

In the end, eight Iu-Mien participants provided information for this study. The gender ratio was four women and four men. The research dialogues occurred in their place of work, home, restaurant, or university center. They were given the choice of the setting in which they felt the most comfortable to share freely in regard to content and time.

Questions That Guided the Initial Dialogues

In order to understand participants' experiences with social workers who may or may not have interacted in a culturally competent manner, it was important to have an understanding of the participants' personal as well as professional backgrounds'. The participants were asked questions regarding their personal history of migration, experiences leading to immigration to the United States, experiences in the United States with communities, institutions, and particularly social service workers, insights into ways social service workers have hindered or advocated assistance, and effective ways to increase social service workers' competency in addressing needs of Iu-Mien individuals and the community.

Once the participants agreed to participate in the study, a background questionnaire was provided to the participants prior to the initial dialogue. The participants were asked to respond to questions that included: Where were you born? What do you remember of your early years? What were the circumstances that brought you to the States? What led you to the field of social services? What is your history in the field of social services? What is your current position in this agency? When were you hired? What population(s) do you serve? The responses to these questions helped in gaining a general understanding of each participant's unique history prior to the initial dialogue.

Under each research question below is a list of questions that were used to guide the dialogue.

Research Question 1: As previous recipients of social services, what have been Iu-Mien social service workers' experiences with non-Iu-Mien social workers?

1. Do you remember any experiences with social service workers outside the United States? Please describe.

104

2. Do you remember any experiences with social service workers within the United States? Please describe. (What did you feel? What were you saying to yourself?)

3. What did the workers do that was most helpful? For you, your family, your community?

4. What did they do that was not very helpful? What caused concern? What upset you, your family, your community? What was your opinion of the experience?

Research Question #2: As practitioners, what were the Iu-Mien social service workers' experiences with non-Iu-Mien social workers?

1. Describe an experience or experiences as a student with a teacher, field placement supervisor, or fellow social work student that demonstrated the workers' cultural competency, or lack of cultural competency.

2. Describe an experience or experiences as a social service worker with a client that may have been affected by your cultural background.

3. Describe an experience or experiences as a social service worker with another social service worker that might have been affected by your cultural background.

Research Question #3: In what way did Iu-Mien social service workers feel non-Iu-Mien social workers were culturally competent?

1. What incident(s) that you have described seem to demonstrate a respect for and understanding of your culture? Why? How?

2. What words from a non-Iu-Mien social worker signified a sensitivity and/or understanding of your culture?

Research Question #4: In what ways did Iu-Mien social service workers feel non-Iu-Mien social workers demonstrate lack of cultural competency?

1. What incident(s) that you have described seem(s) to demonstrate a lack of understanding of or respect for your culture? Why? How?

2. What words from a non-Iu-Mien social worker signified a lack of sensitivity toward and/or understanding of your culture?

Research Question #5: What themes emerged from the Iu-Mien social service workers' experiences with non-Iu-Mien social workers that indicated areas to be included in courses teaching cultural competency in undergraduate social work education?

1. In reviewing your experiences, do you find similarities, a common thread throughout all the incidents?
2. What do you think social workers need to know to increase their cultural competency?
3. How would you like a social worker to approach you about an area that they may feel uncomfortable about or unfamiliar with in regard to your culture?
4. What type of training would you find beneficial to increase your own cultural competency?

Data Collection

The participants were active members of the research team, analyzing the transcripts of their dialogue and providing additions and/or deletions. The process commenced with a dialogue. The procedure that was followed to collect data began with the contacting of agencies to request the distribution of a letter of introduction to Iu-Mien social service workers in the area. Additionally, community leaders were contacted by phone and letter to obtain names of Iu-Mien social service workers in the area. The community leaders were very receptive to the study and assisted with providing individual Iu-Mien social workers with the proposal of project.

Once a social service worker was contacted and a time and setting for the dialogue was arranged, I offered an interpreter if the participant desired. All the participants declined this offer. The participant was then sent a copy of consent form and background questionnaire two weeks prior to the meeting.

Data Analysis

Qualitative data analysis differs from quantitative analysis. In the analysis of material from a qualitative study, "data are not abstracted into summary statistics, but allowed to speak for themselves as manifestations of different aspects of the problem" (Park, 1989, p. 14). The dialogues with the participant(s) are transcribed, followed by interpretation of the data by the researcher and participant(s). Park (1989) related that "research findings do not reveal their social significance as brute facts that speak of themselves; they require interpretation" (Park, 1989, p. 15).

In this study, I transcribed each dialogue and reviewed the content. This allowed an opportunity for me to reflect upon the dialogues and to examine the data for "generative" themes. These are common words or themes that occurred throughout each individual dialogue and throughout the group of participants as a whole. I then provided each participant with a copy of his or her transcript to review and critically reflect upon.

Following sufficient time for me and participants to review the transcripts, through triangulation of the data, a "member check" was conducted. That is, the participant and I discussed our individual interpretations of the data, comparing and contrasting. The participant at that time clarified his or her statements, expounded upon specific areas, and deleted areas that seemed unclear, ambiguous, or were viewed as "inappropriate" for publication due to cultural values.

The participants were co-researchers whose interpretation of the data was considered valid and an instrument of empowerment. From the first dialogue, a second was generated to review the transcripts, assess for themes, sub-themes, and generative words, and to pose new questions. Issues were clarified, and insights were evaluated at a deeper level. During this second dialogue, I continued to "elicit the voice of the participant" (Ada & Beutel, 1993, p. 93).

Park (1989) described the research process following the second, and occasional third, dialogue with the participant. He stated,

The research process reaches a kind of crystallization point where the findings of the investigation are brought together in a systematic fashion at the end. This helps to reveal the extent and the depth of the problem, turning individual miseries into a social mosaic, which is useful in discerning the pattern of social causation. (p. 14)

From the second dialogue, I further analyzed the data for generative themes with the participant in regard to the initial research questions and new areas presented during the research process. The participants were given copies of the analysis to ensure they were provided the opportunity to continue to participate in the process.

Protection of Human Subjects

Prior to the first interview, the participants were provided consent forms, written in English, explaining the study and conditions of their participation. From my Iu-Mien contacts, I have learned that there are numerous forms of written Iu-Mien and many Iu-Mien people read only in Chinese or Lao. Thus, K. Chao (personal communication, September, 22, 2000) did not recommend that the consent documents be written in Iu-Mien, Chinese, Lao and/or Thai. The forms were also read aloud in English. The dialogues were audio-tape-recorded following the written and oral consent of the participants.

If the participant desired, feedback, including quotations, was to remain anonymous in the data collection process and text of the study. The participants were informed as to who would have access to the results and how the data would be utilized. They were informed that they could have copies of the completed report if they desired. The participants were informed of their right to discontinue their participation in this study at any time and/or refuse to answer any questions without any consequences. The participation of each individual was voluntary and she or he was informed that involvement in the study could be discontinued at any time.

In the Iu-Mien culture, there are 12 clans and each clan name is used in the United States as the last name. Additionally, first names designate the birth order of a child. The Iu-Mien communities are collective in nature and many families may reside in the same apartment complex (McDonald, 1997). Due to the nature of clan and first names and the closeness of the community, individuals may be quickly identified through their name. Thus, to protect confidentially and maintain anonymity, the participants were offered the use of letters to identify their names, versus pseudonyms that might cause difficulties for community members who might think they are being identified in this study. However, all of the participants chose to have their legal names used in the text of the study and acknowledgments. Each signed a release form signifying this desire.

Chapter 6

The Participants

The Iu-Mien social service workers who participated in this research provided a wealth of information. Their candid and insightful reflections led to a multi-layered, interlocking mosaic. The richness of the Iu-Mien culture and the strong values of harmony, respect, and cooperation were prevalent throughout the entire research process.

This chapter begins with a table listing all the participants and demographic data (see Table 1). The table is followed by a description of each participant in alphabetical order. All the participants chose to have their actual legal Iu-Mien name included, instead of using a letter as a pseudonym. Each read their "participant profile," providing input as to additions and clarifications.

Five of the participants were born in Laos. All of the participants resided in refugee camps in Thailand. All but one immigrated to the United States during 1979 or the early 1980s in the "second wave" of Southeast Asian refugees. Each participant was sponsored by a church in the United States and resided with or near church members. In the United States, the families were initially isolated from other Iu-Mien families, validating the literature's reports of placement of refugees in nuclear family groups throughout the United States to avoid controversy in communities (Fadiman, 1997; University of California, Irvine, 2000). The participants provided unique narratives of their initial placement in the United States.

Table 1

Characteristics of the Participants

	Name	Age	Gender	Birthplace	Entry into U.S.	Age at Entry	Education
1.	Kim Fahm Chao	27	F	Thailand	1980	5	BS Social Work
2.	Meycho Monica Chao-Lee	25	F	Laos	1982	7	AA Psychology
3.	Sunny Chinn	27	M	Thailand	1991	17	2 years College
4.	Faye Seng Lee	36	F	Laos	1979	14	Portion of AA
5.	Wernjiem O. Pien	36	M	Laos	1982	16	H.S. Graduate
6.	Kao F. Saechao	26	M	Laos	1980	6	BS Social Work
7.	Koy Saephan	31	F	Laos	1979	9	BA English
8.	Chiem-Seng Yaangh	35	M	Thailand	1979	14	MS Social Work

Note: Age and educational status recorded at time of study

The participants are high school graduates or earned a GED. One participant earned an associate's degree at a community college with a major in psychology, two earned bachelor's degrees in social work, one earned a bachelor's degree in English literature, and one recently earned a master's degree in social work and is pursing a doctoral degree in education. As stated previously, the gender ratio of the participants was equal.

A Portrait of the Participants

The following portrait depicts the participants' status at the time of the study.

Ms. Chao

Ms. Chao, age 27 years, was born in Thailand. She immigrated, initially to California in 1980, at the age of five. Her family resided in California for approximately one year before moving to Alabama. Her parents secured employment in assembly work with electrical parts. Ms. Chao related that there were other Iu-Mien families in Alabama who had encouraged the family to move for employment opportunities.

The family returned to California 10 years later to be near other Iu-Mien families. Many Iu-Mien families were resettling in California due to the agricultural businesses and mild climate. Ms. Chao recalled how her family has maintained contact with relatives in Laos through the sending of audio letters, tapes that included verbal communiqués by each family member. This helped to decrease the feeling of physical distance and retain a sense of community and closeness.

Ms. Chao stated that she was the only one in her elementary school in Alabama who was Iu-Mien. She was the first in her family to learn English and was responsible for interpreting for her parents. She is currently fluent in Iu-Mien and English.

Ms. Chao has an earned bachelor's degree in social work and is currently enrolled in a master's degree program in social work. She related, "I have been in the field of social service since I was a kid by advocating for my non-English speaking parents' rights. It was only natural that I continue advocating for people's rights."

Ms. Chao is employed as a workshop facilitator for an agency that serves CalWORKS (Welfare to Work) clients. She facilitates job readiness classes, is a case manager, and works collaboratively with other county agencies to help clients become self-sufficient. She has extensive experience in providing workshops on the Iu-Mien culture, targeting social work students and social service workers. Ms. Chao was instrumental in the completion of a series of three books documenting oral folk tales of the Iu-Mien people.

Ms. Chao-Lee

Ms. Chao-Lee, age 25, immigrated initially to the state of Washington in 1982 at the age of seven. Ms. Chao-Lee recalled living in Laos and related that her father was imprisoned by the Communist government in Laos for the year of 1976, although the war officially ended in 1975.

> They [the Communists] oppressed him. I remember soldiers coming into the house, taking whatever they wanted, food; it was hard, threatening . . . threatening my mom, threatening my grandparents. As little as I was, certain incidents I remember bits and pieces . . . I remember this particular incident where this gentleman came in with a bandana and wrapped it around everyone's face . . . .

Her memories of the war, the refugee camps, and her growing years in the United States provided a framework for her views in regard to the research questions. She described her experiences in the Thai refugee camp, Chiang Kong. She recalled that the children, not the parents, were required to attend school.

> I didn't like it number one because I was Iu-Mien and you are lumped in with everybody, Iu-Mien and Hmong. The teachers don't understand where we're coming from and who we were . . . you go home and you have to do the gardening so your fingernails get dirty. You go to school. They expect you to be spotless and clean and they would get rulers and hit your hand . . . I thought it was unfair.

> And not only that, it was hard to learn what they wanted you to learn. I don't remember exactly what they wanted us to learn, but some was social behaviors, and the alphabet in Thai. It is hard as a seven year old to go into the classroom and catch up with the kids, students who started young . . . being laughed at, [saying] you are so stupid. That was hard.

Ms. Chao-Lee openly provided information on her experiences and was extremely helpful in her recommendations for the teaching of cultural competency.

Ms. Chao-Lee is fluent in English and Iu-Mien. She became interested in the field of social services when she was a senior in high school. She related that she became "Americanized" during her adolescence. She stated that she wanted to use her skills to "teach other people" and thus developed a senior project that was approved by the local school board. Ms. Chao-Lee inferred a lack of support services in the area of mental health for the Iu-Mien community. Thus, her project consisted of volunteering at the local mental health center for approximately 80 hours to assist with translations, outreach, and cultural awareness for staff. Her project was so successful that she was hired, while still in high school, as a contract worker to provide outreach and support.

Ms. Chao-Lee graduated during the middle of her senior year of high school. She was employed to assist with the development of a clinic for outpatient mental health services for the Iu-Mien population. She also worked part time for an in-patient mental health facility. Ms. Chao-Lee then attended community college and became employed by a public health agency.

Upon completion of her associate's degree in psychology five years ago, Ms. Chao-Lee began her present work as a social service worker for an outpatient mental health center. She is currently the Cultural Competency Coordinator. Her duties include interpreting, supervising staff, developing and facilitating cultural competency trainings, providing counseling and home visits, and serving on county committees. Because of her current position, Ms. Chao-Lee works with individuals from diverse backgrounds to ensure that the agency staff provides "culturally appropriate interventions for the consumers." She interacts with other social workers in collaborative efforts with consumers and in consultation with community programs. Ms. Chao-Lee related, "I am very involved in the community as well as educating; I think it is two part. As well as educating the community, on the customs, I am educating my people about the culture here, the system here. It takes both."

Mr. Chinn

Mr. Chinn, age 27, was born in Thailand in 1974. He related that "because of the war, people weren't clear [about place of birth], thus his "official" documents list his birthplace as Laos. He and his family resided outside of refugee camps in Thailand for a period of time and then in a refugee camp. In the camp, Mr. Chinn worked as a translator for the United Nations. He interpreted public announcements in Iu-Mienh and Thai. He also worked in the hospital administering medications and other nursing assistant duties. Mr. Chinn immigrated to the United States in 1991 at the age of 17. He and his family were sponsored by Iu-Mienh families in California.

Upon settlement in California, Mr. Chinn entered high school as a sophomore and in two years graduated with a 3.8 grade point average. He related receiving much support from high school personnel and was able to begin community college full-time upon graduation from high school. During his second year of college, he secured employment in a social service setting. He has worked for several social service agencies that target children, the disabled, refugees, and the elderly. He is currently employed as a family services coordinator for an in-home senior services program.

Mr. Chinn is very active in his community. He has written an unpublished article on Iu-Mienh history and culture. Mr. Chinn has a very open and frank outlook on life. He spoke candidly of his experiences in Thailand and school years in the United States.

> We never have a country. Mienh people moved from China, to Laos, to Thailand, to the U. S., and elsewhere. When we moved to Thailand, people get robbed, people get raped. You know, our possession has been wiped out. They have no mercy. An official hard to be trusted. I'm not saying everyone, but still today, Thailand has lots of immigrant from Laos. But, to my knowledge, they have not accepted any immigrant to be Thai citizen. They don't even have anybody to be in the system. I mean, I love Thailand and I love the country, but that is something I don't really agree with . . . Everything [in the refugee camp] is paid for by the United Nations, you know. People in the camp, a lot of time have unforgotten difficulty put to them by the Thai soldiers. We were kicked, hit, shoot, they would do everything; it's terrible.

That's why I am saying, this nation [United States], people say we have prejudice, discrimination, I would say, it happens everywhere, but I think we have come a long way here. I don't know the future, but I don't feel good when people discriminate me, but you know, maybe that is how the life goes. People do hate you, but they do love you, too.

He visited his homeland in 1998 and related a desire to return again someday to provide support in his country of origin.

Ms. Lee

Ms. Lee is 36 years old and immigrated to the United States in 1979 at the age of 14. Her first place of residence in the United States was in the state of Oregon, moving to Northern California 16 years ago. She described her primary language as Iu-Mien, is fluent in English, and can converse in Lao and Thai. She completed her GED and a portion of her associate's degree.

Ms. Lee provided great detail on the influence of her sponsors and their church in her acquisition of English.

We were sponsored through the church program, even though we were, my brothers and I, not truly a Christian, we had to go to church because the church sponsor us. We loved it. We loved it. We thought it was great . . . you really couldn't perform the rituals, there was no shaman. We were the only families out in that area, far away from any that we known. And so, we, myself, my sister, and my brother, we go to church. Even on weekdays when they have bible study even though we don't understand English and just go. That was a way, of course, to learn English. And so, we just stuck with it and sang songs, you know, we sang the song in the bus, "when you're happy clap your hands."

Ms. Lee became interested in the field of social services through a teacher and employment opportunities. In California, she was offered a position as a bilingual aide in an elementary school. Soon after, she was transferred to a middle school and then a high school. At the middle school, she met an EuroAmerican teacher who was very involved in the Iu-Mien community. He was a strong influence in her career choices.

Ms. Lee's work experience expanded to the field of social services. She is currently employed by a county social service program that administers the California Work Opportunity and Responsibility to Kids (CalWORKS) program, a component of the Temporary Aid to Families (TANF) program. She is an employment and training worker. She experiences much contact with other social workers through Child Protective Services (CPS), Adult Protective Services (APS), the county probation department, and a regional agency that provides counseling and support to CalWORKS recipients.

Ms. Lee and her husband have been very involved in the development of an Iu-Mien community radio show that is broadcast weekly in her community. She is very committed to educating those outside the Iu-Mien community about her culture. She stated that she would like social work students to "be open minded . . . don't be afraid to ask. Try to learn as much as you can. Try to think of how you would want people to treat you if you were a different color and so that you do the same to them." She practices this in her work on a daily basis. Ms. Lee invited me to her home and prepared a delicious, traditional Iu-Mien meal.

Mr. Pien

Mr. Pien is 36 years old, immigrating to the United States in 1982 at the age of 16. He and his family were initially placed in Portland, Oregon. Mr. Pien is a high school graduate. He is fluent in Iu-Mien, Lao, Thai, and English.

Following graduation from high school, Mr. Pien became involved with his community through his work for a northern California migrant education program. He was employed as a secondary school advisor. He assisted junior and high school students; many of his advisees included Iu-Mien students. The interaction with contacts through the schools led to coordination with Iu-Mien community leaders, the leadership group, for several of years. He assisted with school conferences and varying community needs related to education.

For the past four years, Mr. Pien has been employed at a county public health department as a community health advocate. He continues to maintain contact with high school students through this position. Of important note, Mr. Pien recently completed two, two-year terms as the Iu-Mien community leader for his county. Mr. Pien described his duties.

> The Iu-Mien people, wherever we live in city and states, we have community leaders and a few elders. When we have minor problems in the communities, they just go to the community leaders (pause) to solve problems, try to counsel them or just try to work out so they don't have to go to the court, the law enforcement, to try to solve out minor problems.

Mr. Pien's dedication to his community is exemplified by his commitment to providing necessary community programming to reach all potential recipients. He is well known for using his garage as a local immunization clinic and annual flu clinic. The respect he receives from the Iu-Mien community, and the respect he exhibits for his community, is manifested in a commitment to services well beyond his job description. He is a well-respected community leader and advocate for the Iu-Mien people.

Mr. Saechao

Mr. Saechao, 26 years of age, immigrated to the U.S. in 1980 at the age of six. He and his family were placed in the state of Oregon. Mr. Saechao recalled memories of living in a refugee camp in Thailand. He stated, "when you wake up in the morning . . . first you hear the country's national anthem come on, and when you hear it, we were advised to hold still, and not play . . . . " Mr. Saechao is fluent in English and Iu-Mien. He described learning English in the United States when he first arrived.

> I remember going to school. When they [refugees] come over, they go to a school where they just speak English. They don't have kids, like the native kids, speak their native language, assistance to help them. But, when I went, it was just going to class . . . it was a free for all, and I remember it was hard, but somehow I got used to it.

Mr. Saechao's work experience has included the duties of a job coach, bilingual assistant, and work experience coordinator. Currently, he is employed as a service coordinator for a program serving the developmentally disabled. Mr. Saechao views his choice in earning his bachelor's degree in social work as "an opportunity for me to do something good . . . for all the services my family has received." He echoed the words of other participants in regard to continuing to care about his community and family while being torn by his placement in two very different, sometimes conflicting, cultures.

> I was too young to know actually what my parents went through, but as I grow older, I came to realize that my parents, even though I did not appreciate them at a young age, I realize how far they have come. By raising us, keeping us in order and doing all that without adjusting to the traditional norm of American culture. Even though they raised us, I think I still have to watch over my parents even though I am more mainstream than they are. Sometimes I want to break away from that. You know if you do, you think to yourself sometimes, *your parents did this for you. How can you turn your back against them?* But, it is just real hard.

Ms. Saephan

Ms. Saephan, age 31, was born in Laos and resided in refugee camps in Thailand from ages four to age nine. At that time, in 1979, she immigrated to the United States with her family, sponsored by a Catholic Church in Iowa. The family moved to the state of Washington one year later. Ms. Saephan described her experiences in Iowa:

> I think it was very crucial that our family lived there the first year because we picked up English more rapidly. People often tell my siblings and I that we don't have much of an accent. I really attribute this to the fact that we lived there for a whole year before we saw any Mien families.

> Of course for my parents it was very difficult. They thought the rumors in the camp had been confirmed. They thought that American had cannibals. And so, my grandmother really thought the rest of the Mien had been

devoured . . . she went wondering for the rest of the year where the Mien people were.

Four years after residing in Washington, Ms. Saephan moved to California where she earned a bachelor's degree in English Literature. Following graduation from college, Ms. Saephan was employed as an elementary school teacher within several school systems. In addition to her teaching schedule, she was very active in the field of social services as a popular presenter for community and social service agencies on Southeast Asian cultures. Additionally, she worked closely with the Iu-Mien, Hmong, Lao, and Lahu communities in regard to social services, educating about local and federal laws. She was instrumental in the production of a 15 - minute public service video on domestic violence.

Currently, Ms. Saephan is employed as a registered court interpreter, the only Iu-Mien individual in the state of California. Her job entails not only interpreting for the courts, but also educating her Iu-Mien clients in regard to social services. Outside her paid employment, she volunteers her services for speaking engagements, community organizing, and individual assistance in the area of advocacy. Ms. Saephan is fluent in Iu-Mien and English and related that she can understand, but can only converse minimally in Lao. Ms. Saephan exhibits a strong commitment to her community and the education of social service professionals. Her attention to the needs of the oppressed is indicative in the following discussion:

I have been offering free translation services to the Mien families residing near _____ school . . . mostly to families who live at _____ . . . and have worked to organize neighborhood watch meetings held at the school. From all accounts, I would venture to say that this is a high crime neighborhood where many tensions exist.

About a year ago, I stared working actively with families in this neighborhood, both on a personal and a professional level . . . chronic social and criminal issues have resulted in a galvanized effort between the school, the county sheriff, the families and some landlords . . . to tackle

120

problems as a collective . . . . There are many problems between the landlords and their tenants regarding maintenance issues. To make matters works, a county health nurse announced, about three months ago, that two kids have been diagnosed with 20,000 per million level of lead in their bodies. Apparently, there has been lead found in the asphalt. For over four years the county and the landlords have known, according to this nurse. However, with the exception of the two families, other families have not been informed or educated about the lead until this meeting. The fact that nothing has been done is an outrage . . . finally condemned the place with yellow tapes. But, the Mien have little understanding about the negative impact that lead could have.

Ms. Saephan began law school the fall of 2001. She is a recipient of the New Americans scholarship. Her interest is in public policy.

Mr. Yaangh

Mr. Yaangh, age 35, was born in Laos and resided in refugee camps in Thailand for four years before immigrating to the United States in 1979 at the age of 14. He lived in Oregon for 17 years. During that time, he graduated from high school, completed his bachelor's degree in social sciences and worked in the human service field. In Oregon, he initially worked with delinquent youth. Upon moving to California, Mr. Yaangh implemented a family resource center. He recently completed his master's degree in social work and is enrolled in a doctorate program in the field of education. He is currently employed by a school district as an administrator and provides outreach services to schools and communities.

Mr. Yaangh is fluent in Iu-Mien and English and can converse in Hmong and Lao. He became interested in social services due to a "desire to help others, especially disadvantaged populations." Mr. Yaangh poignantly stated his view of the acquisition of cultural competency that related directly to his experience as a refugee.

I think people who begin to become competent are people who have had some experience, some awakening in their life. With me and others like me, because of our experiences of poverty, of being ridiculed, of being looked down upon. I certainly did not feel that we were welcomed in the U. S. We certainly weren't prepared as a country to receive refugees . . . but that caused me to become sensitive to others and to be concerned and compassionate about those that are oppressed, those that are disadvantaged. I am concerned in our district here; I am concerned for all the students. I want to see all students succeed. I don't care what color they are, what race they are, what background they have. When you look at the big picture, if one group or one individual learns and becomes successful, it helps all the others to become successful.

Mr. Yaangh has practiced his values in his professional endeavors. He has been instrumental in the development of many programs that target non-dominant groups including a yearly state conference for Iu-Mien youth that focuses on promoting high school graduation and the pursuit of higher education.

Chapter 7

Critical Reflections of the Participants

The critical reflections of the participants are organized according to the research questions. From the dialogues, generative themes and sub-themes emerged. These are discussed through copious direct quotations. Although this section is organized by the research questions, it is important to note that the dialectic process was not linear. The reflections presented in the dialogues overlapped and were interconnected. The themes became apparent as the dialogues were transcribed and through the second dialogue with each participant. Hall (1993) summed up the process well, stating, "participatory research fundamentally is about the right to speak . . . argues for the articulation of points of view by the dominated or subordinated, whether from gender, race, ethnicity, or other structures of subordination" (p. xvii).

The information presented under each research question is a composite of the first dialogue, the review of the transcripts by the researcher and participant, and the second reflective analysis. Each portion of the research process built upon the previous one, as themes and sub-themes emerged.

In his introduction to the book, *Voices of Change: Participatory Research in the United States and Canada,* Freire (1993) wrote:

Participatory research is no enchanted magic wand that can be waved over the culture of silence, suddenly restoring the desperately needed voice that has been forbidden to rise and to be heard . . . the silence is not a

124

genetically or ontologically determined condition of these women and
men but the expression of perverted social, economic, and political
structures, which can be transformed. [In participatory research] The
silenced are not just incidental to the curiosity of the researcher but are the
masters of inquiry into the underlying causes of the events in their world.
In this context research becomes a means of moving them beyond silence
into a quest to proclaim the world. (pp. ix-x)

During this research, the critical reflections of the participants did seem to move
from a slow introductory process to vibrant exclamations of experiences and
suggestions for change. I utilized italics to emphasize areas that seemed to
highlight the relevant question.

Experiences as Previous Recipients of Social Services: *"Worse Than Dirt"*

The participants provided many different experiences that related to
research question number one. The themes that emerged are organized in the
following order: (a) children as interpreters, (b) assumptions, and (c) adult non-
English speakers: reduced respect/status in EuroAmerican and Iu-Mien culture.

Children as Interpreters

The initial experiences of each participant in the United States involved
helping their family negotiate EuroAmerican society. Many were the first to learn
English in their family and thus, were called upon to interpret. Ms. Chao-Lee was
nine years old when she immigrated to the United States in 1982. Her family was
sponsored by a pastor and his family in the State of Washington. She related:

That was a different cultural experience in itself. I have mixed feelings. I
think that if I could do things over, (pause) I would definitely like to be
sponsored by someone other than Iu-Mien which is what my situation
happened that way. But, I would like wrap-around services where folks
could speak my language. There was no one that knew the culture . . . just
the basic things, stuff like food, you know.

The pastor and his wife did a real good job for us and they tried to help us, but it was really hard having parents who had lost a lot, had lost a sibling, lost their parents, and coming to a new country where *no one spoke the language.*

Mr. Saechao discussed his experiences as translator for parent-teacher conferences. He stated, "the teacher say something, and you tell your parents that you are doing okay. I mean, even though you are struggling. But . . . you didn't want to worry them; there is time when you reverse power and I kind of took advantage of it." The power in the family shifted, and the new responsibility placed on young children was difficult for them. He stated that the Southeast Asian students were viewed by teachers and school administration with no understanding of the inter-cultural differences or needs, categorizing them into one general group. He reflected upon his insights as he gained greater awareness of subtle forms of prejudging.

I think at that point when I was first translating for my parents, I was too young to know what was being projected onto us. But, you know, when you are translating for a regular agency or working with the co-workers, you know how they act or what their reactions would be. Then you start to realize that what is being said or what is being done is not in the best benefit of the other person on the other end.

Children were needed not only to interpret for their parents in school settings, but also in medical situations. Ms. Saephan recalled that she would help her parents make phone calls and read the mail. She stated that due to her skill in interpreting, her parents referred other Iu-Mien individuals to her as an act of generosity. She reported, "they kept saying that 'my daughter will help' so I ended up spending the nights at hospitals."

Ms. Saephan would ride in the ambulance with an Iu-Mien patient and stay in the hospital as long as she was needed. She related that one woman was very desperate, fearing that she would leave her side. She offered Ms. Saephan several thousand dollars (which she did not have) to stay. Ms. Saephan stayed out of duty rather than for monetary reward, stating, "I would leave her side and she would just grip me by the hand, she would hold me really tight." Her fear of the unknown was less painful with Ms. Saephan there to interpret *every* aspect of a medical procedure.

Ms. Chao-Lee related that her father had a bullet in his arm that was lodged during the war. He experienced constant pain, but due to lack of medical insurance, it was not removed when they lived in Washington. In 1987, when Ms. Chao-Lee was a teenager, her family moved to California. Within a year, the pain in her father's arm increased, and through the recommendation of a family member, they sought assistance from the community health center. Ten years after it was initially lodged, the bullet was removed, paid for by Medi-Cal (Medicaid) health coverage as a component of refugee assistance. Ms. Chao-Lee was the interpreter through the entire process.

The stress of interpreting was great for many of the participants. Mr. Chinn's experiences as the primary interpreter for his family continue to haunt him.

> We tried the best. I think, many times, that I did embarrass myself, embarrass my family; people don't like us, they were mean to us. *It's horrible, horrible experience.* And I remember going to Social Security office and the people I believe, they couldn't understand us and they did not have an interpreter, and we just had to go back and go home and read all the handout and go back to the office later. I would try the best to read even though I didn't read much at the time.

In many of the incidents described by the participants, social workers were not available to support or assist in the navigation of community programs. The lack of this support has manifested in long-lasting memories of vulnerability, humiliation, and fear.

Assumptions

The participants provided many examples of social workers making assumptions about their Iu-Mien clients. Mr. Saechao presented an insightful analysis of this human tendency. She stated, "a lot of us [make assumptions] . . . Once you start to realize, there are a lot of assumptions. Even I do a lot of it; I can't help it. It is just my nature of doing it. We got to do it inside, not in front of other people or someone is going to get offended."

Mr. Saechao recalled his experiences as a social work intern during his undergraduate training. As he became acquainted with the social workers at the public social service agency, he became aware of an assumption that all Southeast Asian refugees are "on welfare," using the system rather than earning their own income. He viewed the irony of stereotyping. From his perspective, few refugees were receiving public assistance and were instead experiencing difficulty meeting daily needs due to unemployment and/or low wages in entry-level positions. He stated in the dialogue,

> I wish everyone was on welfare so you would have someone supporting but it is actually, um, actually, um, how shall I put this . . . (pause) It is that most assumptions are not good. That's what I learned. They [stereotypes] are all negative and they are all geared towards groups of individuals, not geared toward a particular individual's achievement.

Differences In Cultural Values

The assumptions in regard to the use of the welfare system were a direct result of the differences in cultural values of EuroAmericans versus the Iu-Mien people. Mr. Saechao noted:

> Iu-Mien marry young and Americans feel that only puts you on social services. Iu-Mien think of the family first, that makes sense. You have kids young. If you don't find a job, you end up on social services. But you get your family established and then make a living, not make a living and then gather your family.

He skillfully articulated the conflict in mainstream, EuroAmerican society between condemning and condoning cultural diversity in the United States:

> [There is the assumption that] Everyone can adjust to norms. But not everyone can adjust. If everyone supports the adjustment to the norms, then we wouldn't have all these different restaurants. I honestly think that we like diversity, but we only like the positive, not the negative.

Language Issues

The participants provided many examples of assumptions in regard to language. A theme that resounded was in regard to all Southeast Asian refugees being viewed within one language category. Mr. Saechao stated,

> A perfect example [was] when I was [in school] there was a new kid enrolled in school and didn't speak English. The secretary would say, 'just call ____, they all speak the same language. They don't know what's going on.' But they do know what's going on. They know what the family needs actually are, it's just they need to find a way to provide that service better . . . rather than just stating that they are different or, (pause) everybody is different.

Ms. Chao spoke openly of her experience seeking Aid to Families with Dependent Children (AFDC). She was a young mother and her husband was completing his university education. She was unemployed at the time and related that the social workers "didn't listen to me . . . right off the bat they just assume that you don't speak English." She was assigned to a Laotian social worker whose primary job was to interpret for the non-English speakers, primarily the Hmong. Ms. Chao stated that she was unable to communicate with her worker as he was described as a limited English speaker and did not speak Iu-Mien.

Ms. Chao related that per her request, she was assigned to another worker. She described the experience of entering the public social welfare facility.

> It's small, it's overcrowded, they don't really treat you, not enough room so a lot of people stand outside and they call out your name and you have

all these people who have to bring their kids there because there is no childcare. I just think it is really bad. All these kids just sitting there.

She related that with the help of her new social worker, who was fluent in English, she was placed in the Greater Avenues to Independence (GAIN) work training program. She was able to complete her academic training as a result of this program. However, Ms. Chao recalled the many assumptions made by her worker during this process.

> I only had contact with her over the phone. That lady just assumed that I was not Iu-Mien. She just thought I was, she didn't, she did not know just from speaking to me over the phone and said you have an appointment with so and so. When we had the appointment, we met with her. She said, "oh, I didn't know you were Iu-Mien, speaking with you on the phone I thought you were American from the way you sounded," and I said, "okay, does that make a difference?" (laughs) "No, I was just really, I just didn't know that you were Iu-Mien"

Through personal reflection, Ms. Chao recalled the initial intake with the social worker. She discussed how assumptions in regard to language impacted not only the process of the intake, but her uncertainty of the worker as someone to trust.

> He [the husband] does this on purpose. We were just sitting there and throughout the whole interview process she was just talking with me and he was just sitting there and didn't say a word and *she just assumed* that he didn't speak English. My motto, you just never assume anything; my motto is that you always ask. She then asked him if he speaks English and stuff and he just kinda started to talk.

> She would ask about him, about his school . . . she would ask me. I don't know why she just talked to me. I think if she would have just asked him he would have talked. Other but from the beginning she just focused her attention on me, from talking on the phone she was "oh great, you speak English."

Ms. Lee recalled applying for Medi-Cal in California. She stated that she was unable to receive Medicaid in Oregon and thus accrued $5,000 in medical bills from the birth of her second child. Upon coming to California, she applied for social services. Ms. Lee stated that her insights into her experience were a result of her fluency in the English language and understanding of EuroAmerican culture. She related receiving Medi-Cal without any difficulty, but at the same time was aware of negative viewpoints of the social worker who granted it.

> If you speak the language and you understand what people ask you and you kinda have a sense of what people are doing. Knowing some sign language and body language, *you kind of know how you are treated. You are more aware, you understand. If you know how society in America works, you do really feel like you are treated, being discriminated.*

Adult Non-English Speakers: Reduced Respect/Status in EuroAmerican and Iu-Mien Culture

The effects of immigration from an Asian society to one with a European foundation were quite profound for Iu-Mien adults, especially elders. Due to language difference, inequity occurred. The status of Iu-Mien adults decreased within not only the Iu-Mien community, but as seen by the dominant EuroAmerican society.

> For my parents, they try to learn English, it is so hard for them to learn and then they just gave up. I know they tried. But, people who don't know them when they talk, think that, "how come you don't learn English? You are too lazy to learn. You are too such and such; you are not putting it into a priority." But, I know they did, and other people don't know that.

For Ms. Chao-Lee, the family was awarded Aid to Families with Dependent Children (AFDC) in light of the difficulty the parents were having in securing employment due to language and skill incongruencies with mainstream EuroAmerican society. Refugee families were provided Aid to Families with Dependent Children (AFDC) as a component of the services provided by the federal government. Ms. Chao-Lee related, "AFDC for my parents and a lot of parents was not good. It depressed them even more." She further elaborated:

> We are independent and we don't rely on anybody, we rely on families. It is very difficult to come here and have to rely on the government. Basically when you are on AFDC, they control your life. They control what you do, what you buy, how you spend your money. And, you're not getting much.
>
> Especially folks who, when I say educated I don't mean like educated academically, they have very high status like a teacher, shamans. They have very high status in the country and they come here and it's like, they're nobody. They're worse, *they're not even respected. They are worse than dirt.* You know, their children get more respect than they do. *Because, the children speak the language.*

For many, the maze of social services was difficult due to the bureaucratic hierarchy and the manner in which services were administered. Ms. Chao provided an excellent example through her father's experience waiting for extended periods to speak to a county welfare worker.

> We were there for hours and they didn't call us. My dad is the type of person who is very gruff (laughs) and we went up there and he was demanding somebody see us now because we were there for three hours. Since he was also working he told my mom waiting in line to get to the window to sign up or whatever. He was pushing his way up the line and I said, "don't do that, you have to wait your turn." He said "no, I'm rushed . . . I'm working"
>
> My brother was 17 and we didn't have any insurance and we needed Medi-Cal. So *he went to the head of the line, he didn't care, he was older,* telling them to move back, he just did that. [He] filled out the forms, saw the worker, and the worker told him he made too much money. He didn't like it because of the way he was treated by workers; he didn't like it.
>
> We just don't like to be kept in the dark, having to wait so long just for something; they send you all this stuff. You fill out the forms and then you have to wait. Then they call you in and it just takes five minutes. He feels it is a waste of his time, sitting there when he could be working. You stand in a line a long time and then when you get up there, they tell you that you

are in the wrong line and don't even help you and you have to start all over!

Experiences as Practitioners with Non-Iu-Mien Social Workers:

"There Was An Assumption . . . . "

The Iu-Mien social service workers provided a wealth of information in regard to their experiences as current practitioners. They seemed very careful in phrasing experiences, tending to focus on positive versus negative interactions. As one participant stated, "for every negative, I must say a positive." This view seemed very reflective of the core Iu-Mien values. The themes that emerged in this area are discussed in the following order: (a) assumptions, (b) Child Protective Services (CPS), and (c) elders-abuse and depression/Adult Protective Services.

Assumptions

Similar to their experiences as recipients of social services, the participants provided examples of assumptions in regard to language that were present in their field of work. Mr. Saechao recalled assumptions relating to the similarity of Southeast Asian cultures, even if language differences were acknowledged.

> I only speak Iu-Mien. But, when I was hired in the ESL area. I was also hired for Lao, which is basically someone who is working with me and don't speak my English. *They [the employer] would assume that I not know the language, but I know the custom.* But, that is a little bit different (laughs). That's why cultural competency is so hard. There are so many things to learn, there are so many diversities, different groups.

He further related that in his current employment, the social workers in the CalWORKS program tended to refer all Southeast Asian clients to him. They seemed to lack the knowledge that his fluency in Iu-Mien did not equate to his ability to speak many of the clients' home languages. That is, there was a lack of understanding that each language is unique and not generalizable to others.

Ms. Chao recalled an incident where colleagues would assume that she could speak and understand all the languages spoken by Southeast Asian refugees. She stated, "I would say, no, no, this person is not Iu-Mien and I don't speak Laos. So, I would have to say and tease and say, 'with a Laotian, it is a long name." And now they tend to ask and say, 'do you know this person, do you?'" Ms. Lee related similar experiences noting, "even if we didn't speak that language, like Laotians, when they see that name they think, 'oh well ____ speaks that language so I will assign it to her.' They have done that to us a lot of the time."

Child Protective Services (CPS)

Inter-cultural incongruencies were quite apparent through the referrals to Child Protective Services (CPS). In the examples described below, it appeared that the families were not consulted during the investigation in a manner harmonious with the Iu-Mien culture. Social workers seemed to lack cultural understanding. Mr. Pien provided insights on the difficulties.

> CPS is probably the group that has some difficulties with any kind of family because it is the kind of situation with children. They have law and regulation. [It] is kind of really, really strict to follow and sometime that communication is hard for some of the Asian families.

> Because, you know, they [CPS] just go by what they hear and the signs and symptoms that are there, because they have law enforcement's perspectives. So it is kind of hard for some of the families. Sometimes if you are upset with them and it is a really minor thing that can become a major problem.

Mr. Chinn elaborated on cultural differences including the health practice of "coining," rubbing the skin with a hot coin causing lesions (Fadiman, 1997).

I am sure a lot of social workers would see that |cultural differences| as neglect, not polite enough. We have a hard time to learn how to sleep on the bed, in a better room, They have a hard time to organize their room. Sometimes they have coining, a bruise and this and that . . . if you knew that it is not |abuse|. The report |is| one thing [that] is scary because they thought all the CPS people were the ones that steal your children. When some officials come to them, they try everything to cover it up. We, Mienh community, don't really believe that taking children away from you is the solution. It's hard. Nevertheless, some parents don't care if their children are being taken away because they have a hard time to deal with those children.

Mr. Pien related that an accident or school incident involving a child might be inappropriately reported to CPS.

Usually CPS, they don't, they don't get two sides of the story before they do anything, taking the victims or do other work. It's kind of hard sometimes . . . they just take the kids or they just take his wife. And then, work out the details later. If a family member thinks it is not a major problem, but in this culture [EuroAmerican] this is a problem . . . It's kind of hard sometimes.

He described an incident that involved a five year-old female falling and injuring herself in her genital area. The child did not alert her parents as to her injuries for several days. When she did complain, her mother immediately took her to a local health clinic. At the clinic, the nurse suspected child abuse and contacted CPS. The child reportedly was removed from her family of origin, without visitation rights for her parents. The family became very distraught. After considerable time, the child reportedly was returned to her family of origin once the allegations were concluded to be unfounded.

Mr. Pien related that the Iu-Mien leadership in his community for many years was working to maintain relationships with police, county sheriff's office, juvenile probation, the chief of probation, and individuals involved in the school system. Thus, these contacts helped to clarify this particular incident and return the child to her home. Mr. Pien stated that the efforts to develop cultural competency within social service networks has been developed in order that "they be open to us |if| something happening to our population and their staff will know and make sure someone will be helping them to interpret or just get a message across before taking action."

Elders – Abuse and Depression/ Adult Protective Services (APS)

Adult Protective Service (APS), like Child Protective Services, is a mandated state program that requires the reporting of suspected abuse of those over the age of 65 years and those considered dependent adults. Dependent adults are aged 18 to 64 who experience "physical or mental limitations that restrict his/her ability to carry out normal activities or protect his/her rights" (Long Term Care Ombudsman, 2001, p. 1). The types of abuse that are mandated to be reported per the Welfare and Institution Code (section 15610.07) in the State of California include physical, financial, neglect, abandonment, isolation, abduction, and mental suffering.

Mr. Saechao described his experience as a social work intern for a county APS agency. He related several cases of reported neglect of Iu-Mien elders. One report that was provided to his supervisors stated that an alleged victim was not given appropriate sleeping space and was sleeping on the floor of the home. He was assigned to investigate. Through the investigative home visit, the elder related that he chose to sleep on the floor because " back in his native country, he wants to sleep on the floor where it is pretty hard, when he can get a rest. He is not used to the cushy stuff, the bed." The case was closed following his report.

In another incident, an elder was reported to be wandering the streets and not receiving proper nutrition and care. She resided with her son and his wife. From the investigation, Mr. Saechao learned that

The mom would go out in the community for a walk or can collecting. She saw this as good exercise and getting in return money, too. Killing two birds. APS said that the son was not buying appropriate food, that she should not have to trash cans. I told the worker to open the frig and see what was in there. There was food in the frig, everything.

The son was upset with APS. There was the assumption that he was not taking care of her. She couldn't talk [hearing impaired], but she could converse with her hands. She was able to get her needs across. There was an assumption because she did not adjust to the norms [of the greater EuroAmerican society]

The traditional Iu-Mien family structure adheres to the cultural value of respect towards elders. The move from Laos and Thailand to the United States has greatly impacted the roles within the family. This was exemplified by Mr. Pien.

Well, usually we live in a big family with many family members. We don't send the elders to nursing homes, rarely, rarely. I don't have anyone in _____ county that the elders live there by themselves like in a nursing home. No. They stay home like my dad, he can't get along, but he stay home. So really [in] our community, family support is very strong still.

He related the some of the elders manifest symptoms of depression due to the change in social structure.

Some are [depressed], because [they] move from countries and lived back there in the mountains and people stay by themselves and don't get involved. It is difficult in the community and in the government and [they] feel they are free and can do what they want. Now it is different and they don't speak the language and the kids, especially the younger generation, don't behave, they don't listen. [They] don't show respect for the parents and that's a problem. They don't work in the field hard like they used to do and they don't the walking and the jogging in the morning.

Mr. Chinn substantiated this view.

Many, many things they have gone through . . . the language, the living, the food, the culture, . . . the transportation. You know, you talk about the daily dressing, the clothing. You talk about communication, the method that we have everything, the environment, the picture of our neighborhood. I say, everything for older people, especially senior, is tough. I feel sorry for them. I, too, have not easy time to adjust. But, I think I am a little more lucky that I am able to manage to the best possible.

Lack of Understanding or Respect of Iu-Mien Culture by

Non-Iu-Mien Social Workers: *"They Occupy A Whole Different World"*

For many participants, this was the most difficult area to discuss. As stated previously, the Iu-Mien culture values harmony and cooperation. Public criticisms of others is not considered an appropriate topic for discussion. The themes that emerge from the dialectic process are discussed in the following order: (a) lack of affirmation by colleagues, (b) cultural differences in values and communication, (c) conflict with loyalty-agency versus community, and (d) crime. In general all these areas reflected the view of "the other" that was well stated by Ms. Lee, " they would make comments about '*your* culture' and who you are."

Lack of Affirmation by Colleagues

Ms. Chao-Lee discussed the lack of acknowledgement of her traumas by co-workers. She related that the "Secret War" in Laos was indeed still an unknown for many of the social workers she knew. She recalled experiences where clients who had experienced a loss of a loved one were, at times, negated by the worker. As presented in the beginning of chapter one, Ms. Chao-Lee stated:

> It used to be we they come in, when they come in they talk about why I lost my husband in the Mien war, [social workers would say] "they are too young, what are they talking about? Well, there was a war, but what war? *You're lying to me."*

Ms. Chao-Lee recalled, "staff have actually said to me, 'you are lying to me, there was no such war.'"

Cultural Differences in Values and Communication

Many of the participants said that they were seen by co-workers first as a colleague [i.e.. mainstream American] and secondly, as an individual from the Iu-Mien community. Due to this perception by co-workers, areas where the workers lacked cultural competency were presented in a clear and sometime quite insensitive fashion. Although the participants were glad that their colleagues asked questions to clarify inaccuracies or misconceptions about the Iu-Mien culture, on many occasions they seemed to feel ambivalent about the manner in which the colleague presented their misunderstandings.

Ms. Chao was well integrated into her agency and provided an open forum for non-Iu-Mien social workers. She was frequently asked questions by co-workers in regard to areas of cultural uncertainty, stating "they come and ask me, 'is this what it is supposed to be?' I'll tell them that "this is from the way I see it; this is what they do.'"

Dietary Habits

In one incident, a colleague came to Ms. Chao-Lee and said, "...I went to some folks' house and they were eating some weeds." She recalled the event stating,

> What I tell them is it that they aren't weeds, they're vegetables. *And guess what, maybe a thousand years ago your ancestors were eating the same things.* Now, since there is so much material, you go to the store. But for them, they have been here for less than twenty years. They're very used to growing their own crops, and when that's not going good, they don't have a sprinkling system, they don't have a well. They rely on the rain. If there is no rain, then the food is not going to grow, and they have to go out to the wilds and pick whatever they can find eat and eat it and hope that it is not poison. "This plant didn't poison me, it was good, it was edible," and they rely on that.

Ms. Chao-Lee was thorough in the manner in which she educated her colleagues, but at the same time found the workers' reactions aggravating. In reviewing the initial transcript in regard to this discussion, Ms. Chao-Lee related that she previously would eat alone in her office to avoid comments from staff about her foods. Presently, she offers tastes to other workers and they have reported a desire to make the foods at home, seeming surprised that the greens are from common plants that "grow out in the fields." Ms. Chao-Lee was successful in her attempts to educate the social workers in regard to varying cultural foods and to develop their appreciation for something that at one time seemed to belong to "the other," one inferred as "less than."

Mr. Yaangh described an incident that was a result of growing opium in a Iu-Mien community garden. The plant is used as a spice, and the leaves are use in a type of salad and to wrap ground meat. The plant is cultivated before the flower blooms, thus it not grown for intended illegal use. In this incident, the police became aware of the plants and arrested Iu-Mien community members. Mr. Yaangh related that through the help of Iu-Mien people who were fluent "enough" in English to explain the misunderstanding, the individuals were released that day. However, Mr. Yaangh stated that for those who were arrested "it was shameful."

Ms. Chao-Lee described another incident involving a fellow social worker that said to her, "Someone called me, knocked on my door and wanted to pick my bamboo." Ms. Chao-Lee stated that she said to the social worker, "I would have too if I had seen your bamboo; I would have walked to your door and asked if I could pick it (laughing). I would have offered to pay for them." Ms. Chao-Lee reflected upon her perceptions of the lack of cultural competency in social workers relating, "it's just a lot of misunderstanding, a lot of not knowing."

Early Marriage/Childbirth

As discussed in chapter three, the Iu-Mien culture does not view early childbirth and/or marriage as a stigma. Additionally, divorce is not viewed as an easy option when conflict occurs in a marital relationship. Ms. Chao recounted that she is frequently asked about this aspect of her culture and responds to inquiries by

. . . always emphasizing with them, to a lot of people, that the marriages are not arranged, people have choices. They had a choice, they wanted to marry, and it is not like the parents are "you know want, you have to marriage this person." They don't do this; this is someone who you are having a lasting relationship and maybe you should reconsider. If they say "yea" then they take the necessary steps because it's something that the community prides itself on, daughter that might get married and it is a big affair for them.

Further elaborating on the view of marriage and the family unit, she said,

It's not just that the husband and wife, it is two sides of the family coming together . . . it's a community thing, too. That's why they frown on divorce; it's a lot of people. It's hard, especially when there are kids involved. *With domestic violence they say, "forget about the family." But, it is not that easy.*

Ms. Chao-Lee provided her perspective of early marriage in the Iu-Mien culture and the overall divorce rate in the United States. She spoke openly of her support of the Iu-Mien culture stating,

A lot of times we always say, "that poor girl she got married so young." Well, why not look at it when you say "that poor girl" [that] we don't have very much divorce rates. In this county I think there are only like twelve so far, only twelve people out of the fourteen, fifteen hundred and that's been in the last three years. Prior to the last three years, you don't hear of divorce. When you get married young, you are forced to fall in love, get to know each other. You've been told that when you get married, you are not going to get a divorce. So, it's not right to say "you poor thing." Yes, it is hard, but you get a lot out of it, especially if you know how to communicate with your in-laws and know the system. You gotta know the system, how the Iu-Mien system works.

Social customs. Ms. Chao discussed the relationship Iu-Mien clients developed with their non-Iu-Mien social workers. Several social workers in her agency had cultivated relationships with their clients through several years of maintaining their cases. Ms. Chao stated that the workers were "kinda used to the family . . . what is going on . . . the surroundings." However, she described incidents that exemplified a lack of knowledge of social customs and appropriate ways to address clients to learn of their culture.

Many of the clients' parents or elders were home alone for long periods of time while the children attended school or worked. Ms. Chao related that one way to combat loneliness and isolation was to entertain guests. Additionally, many Iu-Mien families relocated to housing subdivisions or apartment complexes. These moves seemed to be attempts to replicate the villages in Laos.

Ms. Chao discussed the visit of a social worker during a housewarming party for one family. The worker, upon her return from the visit asked Ms. Chao, "Could you answer this? There were a bunch of men smoking out of a . . . I don't know what you would call it . . . (pause) [water pipe] . . . what was it that they were smoking? I just saw all these older men outside, just sitting there smoking." Ms. Chao stated that she explained the custom of smoking tobacco that was prevalent among elders. The social worker responded to her with, " I didn't know what it was and, and *it just seemed really weird to me* . . . . " The use of the word "weird" was seemingly stated without insight that the worker was describing her reaction to Ms. Chao's own culture.

Ms. Chao recalled another experiences that a colleague had recounted to her in regard to a home visit with an Iu-Mien family. The social worker was to meet with the daughter who was the client. Upon entering the property, the father was her first contact. Ms. Chao related that the social worker described the scene:

> There is a man sitting by the doorway [much intonation] and with a chicken (laughs) and he was doing something. She said, "I wasn't sure if I was to go in the doorway and I was just standing there and he told me to come in . . . he was really nice and he just kept talking to me and I wasn't sure if I should be there."

The daughter was not home and the social worker became perplexed as to the appropriate manner of addressing the father. When the worker returned to the agency and asked Ms. Chao, "What was he doing?" She explained to her, "I said, 'it's okay, they are really nice and they want you to be there, that is why they are doing that.'" From Ms. Chao's perspective, the cultural differences seemed to cause the social worker such anxiety that she was unable to perform her duties during the home visit.

Ms. Chao-Lee provided another example of a social worker making a home visit to a Iu-Mien family. The family members reportedly provided a stool for the worker that was reserved for guests. It was placed in the middle of the room and the family sat around her. The social worker related becoming uncomfortable and was unsure as to the proper etiquette. She came to Ms. Chao afterwards and Ms. Chao told her,

> You know, when they have a guest come, they just go all out. If this is all the furniture and you have somebody come by, no matter how comfortable you are, you would always get up . . . give this person your chair. And if you are eating at the time somebody come by, you're always inviting them to eat with you, even if they do not want to eat. They sit with you and talk with you, they don't want you to be sitting in the middle and be waiting for you while you're eating, with them eating. And this is just what they do.

Ms. Chao-Lee provided another example that related to the difficulties that ensue when cultural values and communication styles are not understood. She spoke of an incident when she was asked to come to the jail as a representative of her agency. Unbeknownst to her, the individual who was detained was a client of hers. She was also unaware that she was being summoned to the jail not to evaluate for mental health services, but to provide interpretation.

Ms. Chao-Lee related that she had been previously trained as a court interpreter, but had not maintained her training for several years. Thus, she did not feel competent as a court interpreter at this time. She related that she explained this to the officials at the jail, but was asked that she continue to interpret regardless of her concerns. Ms. Chao-Lee felt compelled to interpret to the "best of my abilities." Upon completion of the interpretation, Ms. Chao-Lee related that she apologized to the detainee stating, "I hope I have done the best I could."

She related to this researcher that she actually thought she had performed very well, but that she apologized out of respect for the individual and in part, because of the cultural values of respect and humility. When Ms. Chao-Lee returned to her work setting, she related this story to her supervisor who reportedly had great difficulty in understanding why Ms. Chao-Lee felt compelled to apologize. The supervisor felt that this was not appropriate and alluded that there was a possibility that the apology might have tainted the individual's testimony and, in turn, could result in a legal case involving her agency.

Ms. Chao-Lee and her supervisor discussed this incident in much length and could not seem to come to a mutual understanding of Ms. Chao-Lee's concerns in regard to interpreting and apologizing. Thus, she and her supervisor agreed to discuss it the next day after they re-evaluated the situation. Ms. Chao-Lee reported that the next day her supervisor seemed to have gained insight and stated that he understood why she apologized due to cultural values. He was then supportive of her behaviors.

In all the examples presented, the Iu-Mien social service workers were very gracious in sharing the culture with colleagues when requested. However, the manner in which they were approached seemed to lack cultural competency. The Iu-Mien social service workers appeared to be viewed as "others," those outside the Iu-Mien culture, and thus care was not given to the manner in which questions were addressed. An Eurocentric focus seemed to prevail, as was disregard for the richness of non-European cultures.

Conflicts with Loyalty-Agency Versus Community

Work within one's own community while being employed in a public social service agency can lead to conflicts. The Iu-Mien community in Northern California is described as a very tight network of families. Working for a social service agency at times seems to compromise Iu-Mien customs and to cause conflict as the two cultures clash. Mr. Saechao stated this well:

> That's why sometimes it is hard for me to work on these cases with Southeast Asians because I know them so well and I know what is appropriate and what is not appropriate. And then, even when it is appropriate in our community, but not to U.S. customs, how do I tell them that? How do I justify that it is not okay. Do I just not do anything, not cover myself on this end [as a social service worker]? Or should I just let them know what is going on? *Turn my back on them? You know, my community.*

He related that he resolved this conflict by choosing not to accept cases involving individuals from the Iu-Mien community. The boundaries were too skewed and caused much emotional distress for him and his community. Mr. Saechao discussed the assumption when he worked for Child Protective services that he could help a person because of his nationality. He stated that this rang true for some of his clients, also. There seemed to be that assumption by staff and clients that all Southeast Asians are alike.

Mr. Chinn related that he dealt with this conflict by talking with the clients about his various roles. He would say,

> Just pretend that I don't know you and you can answer me. If you don't feel comfortable, right now I am wearing the hat from my work. I am not wearing the hat from Saturday or Sunday where I know you.

Although he tried to focus on this technique, he stated, "It is tough to separate yourself." Mr. Pien noted the fine line between the values of a social work professional and workers' personal values. His evaluation of the common quandary in regard to the profession as an extension of the person is presented below:

> I am social service worker. If I just leave my job and don't pay any attention to the community and then what? Sometimes hard and the people

will say, "what are you doing?" Say, "my job is this and this, helping people." Well sometimes people need your help [outside of work].

Since she is Iu-Mien, Ms. Chao related that she was frequently asked about other workers' clients who were Iu-Mien. For example, if a client did not show up for an appointment or had specific difficulties, she would be asked if she had any knowledge as to the case that might shed light on the behaviors or areas of concern. This caused a conflict in regard to her commitment to her community, her employer, and the social work code of ethics. Confidentiality, professionalism, and community values were several areas that juxtaposed.

Ms. Chao stated that a non-Iu-Mien social worker had a female client who was missing appointments. The non-Iu-Mien supervisor asked Ms. Chao about her colleague's client. Ms. Chao related:

> I said, "with the Iu-Mien people, they tend to be more compliant, because if they have an appointment, they tend to make that appointment because it says that you have to come."

> So, I say that I will check and see if this person is already working or has some other issues. Because, I know that personally in the community that something is going on with this family. She [the worker] had to call and apparently the client was already working. She got a job and that's why she didn't show up.

Ms. Lee described similar experiences stating,

> I have told them that some of them are people who I know; I don't feel comfortable seeing them, in my culture. The clerical is the one who actually opens the case and does the registration. And, they know me pretty well, everyone knows me, so they would come and ask for comments and ideas and suggestions. Whether I know that person, whether that person speaks English or not, enough where they can communicate in a regular employment setting or by employment training workers.

Mr. Chinn discussed the conflict he experienced working for Child Protective Services.

It's hard . . . even if you really be sure to tell them, "I am not here to take away your children. I am here to help you. " That's how I separate myself. I can't even imagine a CPS social worker [detaining children], I would have, (pause) the community would change my name. They would know me as the "children stealer." It's tough.

He related that he worked to resolve the conflict by emphasizing that he was not the client's "enemy." He focused on his role as an advocate for the family, to provide services, not to separate parents from children. Mr. Chinn stated, "there is a clear message that needs to be said to them" in regard to his commitment to the community and his role in his employment.

Crime

Crime in the form of both domestic violence and offenses committed by Iu-Mien youth appeared to be perceived through an ethnocentric lens by the non-Iu-Mien social worker colleagues. The examples below were very indicative of the stories told by many of the participants.

Domestic Violence

Ms. Chao described an experience in which she was an invited presenter on the Iu-Mien culture for 150 social service workers. Following her talk, she was asked by a male, EuroAmerican social worker in the audience if the Iu-Mien community condoned domestic violence, specifically spousal abuse. The social worker asked her, "Do you guys as a community think it is okay for a man to hit a woman?" Ms. Chao related that she responded by stating:

You know, for the community perspective, a lot of the elders do see that as okay because, let's say, for instance, if in a couple, the women goes out and has an affair, the man, the husband, will see fit to him to do whatever is necessary to save face for his family. Because the woman has gone out and done this, everybody knows, the whole community knows.

The man then stated, "so you think it is okay for a man to hit a women?" She responded:

> If it means that he has to do that, and if the wife is not going to do it anymore, and they reconcile to be together, then that's what it takes. That is what the elders believe. *It is a complicated issue in my culture.*

Note that she did not mention the elders again until the end of her second remark. This could be interpreted as a sign of respect, speaking for the community first from a collective orientation.

Ms. Saephan related the difficulty in colleagues' understanding why a victim of domestic violence was unable to recall dates of specific incidents. She related a lack of understanding of the cultural differences in regard to Iu-Mien society and mainstream EuroAmerican.

> I would say, well, is it surprising that this woman doesn't keep dates when she is being battered? Because of her background, she has never been in a classroom setting, never been exposed to any form of education, the only time she uses a pen is to sign her name. Is it any surprise that a women coming from this background and this experience, that she wouldn't keep dates that she was battered?

Ms. Saephan further elaborated on experiences of Iu-Mien women with social workers who became frustrated when the women did not leave their families and continued to sustain abuse. She stated:

> They [social workers] get frustrated and they don't understand why [the women stay]. They pass off these people as just not willing to try very hard, but actually they are drowning in a pool of dysfunctionality. I think that it is a very difficult area to try to get them [Iu-Mien women] to change when *they occupy a whole different world.* In the American system . . . everyone finds out about it, [and in the case of rape] the issue of

marriagability . . . the girl's ability to get married to a man, a respectable man, in her own community [becomes paramount].

Youthful Offenders

Ms. Lee provided an example of a concept commonly used in the field of social psychology, the illusory correlation. This is an assumption that two unrelated events are related. When an individual is from a non-dominant group in the society, it may be assumed by others that events that happen outside their realm, in regard to others from their community, are related to them. Stereotypes are a form of the illusory correlation. Horowitz and Borden (1999) state, "if both a minority and majority group have the same negative trait . . . the negative behavior will be more distinctive when paired with the minority as compared to the majority group" (p. 202). The following case described by Ms. Lee exemplifies this:

> You know how we have teenagers that get in trouble? Say that you have a Caucasian that breaks into a car, carjacking. It is on the news and not a big deal. But, if you had an Asian kid that did that and it came out on the news, it is a big deal. You show up to work, people ask, "was that your people . . . was that someone you know? Was that a family member?" They make comments like that all the time.

Ms. Lee related that if the offender was EuroAmerican, she did not observe similar comment made to EuroAmerican social workers.

Cultural Competency of Non-Iu-Mien Social Workers: *Respect-Do Not Assume*

The participants in the study also provided examples of non-Iu-Mien social workers who exhibited cultural competency. They discussed social workers who provided services to them and their families, and those who were mentors. The participants each discussed social workers who encouraged them to pursue the field of social services. Mr. Pien discussed the reactions of non-Iu-

Mien social workers when Iu-Mien workers have intervened and said, "this is part of our culture."

> Some is really open. A lot of people are really aware of different populations and diverse culture sensitivity. They learn a lot and a lot of people know what is going on because we have this New Year event . . . [we] try, try to get more and more community [to know] what is going on.

Each participant provided an example of a mentor who had encouraged him or her to pursue the field of social services. Mr. Saechao provided an example of a social worker who expressed interest in his life, encouraged him to obtain higher education, and to not "waste my life around not doing anything." He related, "all it takes [to be culturally competent] is someone to be sensitive, open. [They] don't have to know everything . . . [she was] how I would want a role model."

Ms. Chao-Lee was a teenage mother and received services from a county teen pregnancy prevention program. She was visited regularly by a social worker who provided support for the completion of high school and parenting needs. Ms. Chao-Lee related that prior to the initial dialogue, she had met with her previous social worker.

> I was telling her she was so wonderful and I think that she succeeded because she went into our community. She was not afraid to talk to your parents. She was not afraid to talk to you or your spouse or your family members. She walked in; she has very high self-esteem, but yet when she walked in *she gave a lot of respect to the elders which that can do a lot.* You know, when you get that respect, you can do anything and you can bend the rules. It's when you don't have the respect from the head of the household, the elders, no matter how hard you try, no matter what you do, you are seen as the evil person.

Ms. Chao-Lee elaborated, reflecting on the behaviors that helped the social worker to gain the respect of her family. She described the social worker as smiling frequently and offering her services to the mother of the client stating,

"I'm here to work with you and your daughter. What can I do for you?" The social worker seemed flexible in her manner of conducting home visits. Ms. Chao-Lee related:

> If I was in the garden, she went in the garden with me. She did what I did. If I was picking the plants, she picked the plants with me. *So, that was very well respected by my husband's family.* They don't just see this person as an outsider, as an agency person to get her ten dollars or whatever. They see as a person that really cares, that's trying to do good, trying not to get us in trouble. Because, the way that we look at it is that the person is okay; what does this person really want, and what can they do for us?

Ms. Saephan recalled a social worker that visited her mother on a consistent basis when they resided in Washington. She described the worker as a "source of comfort" because "she was available simply to listen to her concerns." Ms. Saephan related that the social worker was "someone my mother could speak to" because, due to cultural aspects, she was unable to share her feelings with her husband.

Recommendations for Social Work Education

The participants provided many recommendations for the development of increased cultural competency in social work students and current workers in the field. Many spoke of the need for social workers to enter the field with an understanding of the depth of involvement the work entails. Ms. Saephan worded it well:

> I think that they have to be receptive and have compassion. I think there are times when people get into the field of social work and don't fully understand the extent of the passion that is required. Being a social worker is like being a social engineer. You are trying to get people to change certain aspects of their life in order to fit with the laws of this country. This is an area that requires good people skills in helping others to resolve problems with which they are confronted. If social workers don't have the tools to work with a certain group of people, they become easily

frustrated. And, they become easily drained. After a while they become disinterested.

She described the characteristics necessary in light of the intensity of problems a worker encounters. Ms. Saephan stated, "You have to be a person who is willing to be empathic. Unless you have those very basic feelings or desire to work, I think it will be very difficult."

The participants' ideas for increasing cultural competency in social workers resounded with four primary themes. These were: (a) internships and cultural immersion, (b) respecting varying cultural norms, (c) outreach and communication, and (d) asking questions to combat assumptions.

Internships and Cultural Immersion

Mr. Saechao focused a great deal on the idea of an "opportunity for hands-on exposure because you can't read about it and comprehend it until you physically start doing the tasks. " He promoted cultural immersion through internship because,

> Then you start to realize what is important to them, what are top priorities, needs and wants. Different people, different groups have priorities. Hands on give them opportunity to maybe handle one of the groups from a different background and they will, hopefully, teach them the knowledge and experiences that they had.

Mr. Saechao stated that "in order to learn cultural competency, [you] first need a job in public social services with all sorts of groups."

Ms. Chao-Lee elaborated on this idea stating that social work educators might cancel class one week in order for the students to attend a cultural event such as a New Year celebration. The students would be required to write a critical reflection about their experience. She stated that as a supervisor, she mandates her staff to attend community events on a routine basis. In the past, she arranged for staff to spend a day in the Iu-Mien community. She recalled,

We went to the neighborhood. There was a wedding that day. [I] took them around the neighborhood, showed them their lifestyles here are pretty much like Laos. Families go into people's homes without knocking, they knew each other, they earned the trust, and how the wedding was prepared, the food, how it was cooked, the ceremony, the wedding vow, how it was done. From there, I had them put a basket on the back, and then carry it, walk down the hill, cross the creek, to go to the gardening, (laughs) pull weeds (laughs), rank them, because that is what they, they had to do all that stuff (laughs). [Then] walk up to the park and had lunch there. It was Iu-Mien traditional food, nothing else. They had to use chopsticks; if they didn't, too bad! (laughs)

The outcome from this activity seemed unequivocally positive from the feedback she received from the staff. She stated, "that's what really helped to open their eyes and see when their clients come in. The clients talk about their home situation; it helped them to understand it. Seeing it was much more than words."

Ms. Lee related providing similar opportunities for her co-workers and the community at large. She opened up her home to educate social workers about her current life and, as she stated, "how we used to live our life." She felt that the majority of those she temporarily immersed in her culture found it "fascinating . . . what we went through, the struggles we had. And, so that helped a lot." She continued, "when we would have our traditional occasions, special occasions, I would invite them to my house or my in-laws house. I would invite them for like New Years . . . a free admission party, celebration. All the people that goes there would dress in Iu-Mien [and the guests would] have a buffet."

Ms. Chao-Lee viewed her role as an educator. The development of cultural competency included the sharing of examples and life stories. There were seen as vital to increase understanding by non-Iu-Mien social workers. Mr. Saechao stated that sharing would allow workers "to realize we are trying to adjust to the norm; we are not trying to kind of disrespect the norm. We are trying to keep our norms and adjust to theirs as well."

Respecting Varying Cultural Norms

The participants unanimously related that social work students need the basics of respecting the cultural norms of all groups. Mr. Saechao stated, "if you want workers to be culturally competent, don't impose traditional norms and values of society onto others." He further elaborated on this:

> A worker's first impression determines the client's trust and willingness. With all new clients, put yourself in the consumer's place, try to feel they can count on me. The CalWORKS quotas, certain number that you have to meet – *you can't meet the quota with people, you can with merchandise.*

Ms. Chao-Lee elaborated on the need to be aware of ethnocentrism to gain an acceptance of cultural differences. She described two ways that a social worker might approach an interaction with a client from the Iu-Mien community. The first example was that of the worker with an assimilationist view. The second was of a worker whose desire to be cultural competence causes him or her great anxiety. The client then feels uncomfortable and in turn, wants to rescue the worker.

> If you go not trying at all [a person would state], "We'll I'm an American. I was born and raised here. Yes, she is a Iu-Mien, but she is in my country right now. If I can do it, they can do it. If my ancestors came here a hundred years ago and they have problems, too." My family is expected to assimilate into this culture. They have to . . . [because the social worker says] "get them out there and make them, force them to."

> The other one is when they try so hard [and say] "I can't do this, I can't do this." They can't be themselves; they are shaky. They get so nervous. If they are coming to see, I can't read her or his mind. [I think as the client] What are they trying to do? What do they want from me? How can I help them? It's not clear.

Ms. Chao-Lee's advice for social workers was to "just be yourself." During the reflection of the initial dialogue, she stated,

Our needs may not be the same, but how we feel how another person treats us is the same. The tone of voice, hurt feelings, they are the same. Be sensitive to others . . . don't focus on the right thing; you will be cold. Don't be so careless either. By not working with a certain culture, you just say, "you need to teach me and if I do things that are offensive, tell me. I don't want to offend you." It's okay to ask; we don't know all the answers.

Ms. Chao-Lee considered respect of the culture and individual as paramount, stating, "respect for us is a big thing . . . respect, loyalty, and honor." She stated, "What you gotta do is smile a lot, earn their respect. However you do it, just earn their respect. [Then] no matter how big the mistake is, you're forgiven. And they will know that you try." Mr. Saechao agreed with Ms. Chao-Lee's perspective:

Just smile and nod because that is the universal sign of approval . . . when you smile and nod and say "yea," they somehow know that even though we don't understand, we're there, we are listening, we are trying. We are not trying to turn our backs against whomever the person is we are trying to help.

Ms. Chao spoke of her desire for non-Iu-Mien workers to understand the values of the Iu-Mien culture. The values of harmony and collectiveness would lead to positive social work-client relationships. She stated:

I tell this and I joke with my husband all the time. You know the Southeast Asian people are really compliant. You know, they don't really want to get in trouble. If a person says you have to be here, they always show up. The other clients don't show up. No matter if they have to do something that day they will totally come to that meeting because you got this letter that says you have to show up for this thing and do this and this . . . [because] they said you have to do this.

Outreach-Communication

Ms. Chao-Lee felt that social workers needed to demonstrate cultural competency not simply through academic study, but by their actions. She related:

No matter how many social service agencies that say they are open to everybody, nationality or creed, you can say that, you can have that, *but unless you are really out there, outreach, no one is going to come to you.* You got to go out . . . you need to go to the community leader.

The director of her agency secured funds for a community outreach program. These funds were used to hire social workers from varying cultural groups to develop clinics in cultural communities and provide specialized services for the elders.

Mr. Pien reiterated the need to include the community in the work with the Iu-Mien client. He stated, "you have to sometimes pay attention to what is going around you . . . family is the first, but community is still [important], sometimes you have to be open to it." Mr. Chinn related that attending cultural events in the Iu-Mienh community would aid in the development of relationships. He emphasized that a social worker needs to "believe in" the culture, that is, have a commitment to the community.

I think the best way to practice delivering your service is to have someone in the community that the client knows them from the same culture. If possible, have one culture worker accompanied with a non-culture worker to meet with the client. After a trust is built, the services should be able to deliver. You want the community to know you so that they can trust you. Go out to the community event. Visit people. Be known to the community. You can't from the bushes just jump out and say, "hey there is this service." I think that would be a very big mistake.

Many of the recommendations seemed applicable for use with groups from all cultures. Mr. Saechao recommended the use of an interpreter for home visits. Ms. Chao related advice that initially might seem very elementary and obvious to even a novice social worker. However, these words were the outcome of several interactions with social workers that felt uncertain as to appropriate action such as the ones described previously in this chapter. Ms. Chao's recommendations were:

If they offer you a seat, just take it and sit down and then, then obviously if she has been there a couple of times, the parents will know who she is and why she is there. Once she is sitting she can say, "is this person home?" and ask about her. If she is not there, just kind of say, "well, tell her I came by " and then "tell her to call me or I will call her" or something.

Ask Questions to Combat Assumptions

Ms. Chao-Lee related that sometimes the most obvious technique to gain cultural competency is the one least used. She viewed this as a result of fear.

As social workers, don't get scared when there are a lot of family members. Don't get scared when there is a lot of noise. Don't get scared when a person has red marks on their body. *Ask them.* They'll tell you. *Ask them*, "why are there red marks on your body?" "Oh well he was sick and for us we relieve the tension and the stress, do coining." *Always ask.*

Ms. Lee reinforced this view of fear as a barrier to the clarification of assumptions. She explained the importance for social workers to enter the Iu-Mien community with an "open mind."

Don't be afraid to ask. Try to learn as much as you can. Try to think of how you would want people to treat you if you were a different color and so that you do the same to them. You will get it back. What goes around, comes around. And, *don't be afraid.*

Mr. Pien focused on the need to become acquainted with the community. He stated, " Just *go ask directly* to the family . . . know people that work with the community. Talk to them or talk to the community leaders." Ms. Chao-Lee felt that to resolve the barrier erected by assumptions, the social worker needed to interact with clients to provide a forum for dialogue, empowering the client as well as the social worker. She discussed the value of community and support within the Iu-Mien culture and how it is manifested in the United States. One result of the value of cooperation may lead to a misunderstanding by social workers that are not acquainted with the culture and do not ask when they are concerned. Ms. Chao-Lee stated,

> If you go into a home, a two bedroom apartment with twenty people, maybe shabby but they have nice cars, don't judge, don't judge them on that. Because, they rely on each other. Car is more important to us than it is the house. We are used to living in huts, lived in dirt. So whatever it means to us, the professionals, to them it is a luxury. That vehicle, four or five families put money together to buy that vehicle. You have to get that. *They put money together* and they use the cars. Or they buy salvage title cars . . . they pay less than half, you know.

Ms. Chao reinforced this stating, "I just think that automatically from the beginning *don't assume* . . . I like it when they ask. " She elaborated,

My motto is, no assumptions. That's just what I am working on. I used to do that a lot, not just with the Iu-Mien, with anybody else, I was assuming something about the person and then, it turns out that I was pretty wrong. I always ask questions; *if you don't know, ask.*

CHAPTER 8

Summary:

"Our Pain is Because of Grief"

The purpose of this study was to describe the experiences of Iu-Mien social service workers with non-Iu-Mien social workers when they were clients and currently as practitioners. The goals of this research were (a) to gain insights into the ways social workers have displayed cultural competency and/or a lack of cultural competency and (b) to generate recommendations for content areas for inclusion in courses teaching cultural competency in undergraduate social work education.

Through dialogic interchanges with the participants, this study integrated the voices of eight Iu-Mien social service workers in order to enrich the understanding of cultural competency and more urgently, understand the need for change. It was a rare and valuable opportunity for this researcher's enlightenment and growth. Many of the participants were excited about the research since very little is written about the Iu-Mien people. They were receptive to the publication of these findings, desiring that their voices be heard to help to develop an understanding of their culture and experiences in the American society. It is my hope that the participants' open and insightful dialogues will be reciprocated by a "nonacademic presentation of findings in a format that is accessible to the community . . ." (Petras & Porpora, 1993 p. 112), the community of not only Iu-Mien individuals, but those unfamiliar with their culture and experiences.

The study brought forth an awareness for the participants of their past and current experiences, and, in turn, ideas for increasing cultural competency in social workers. Hall (2001) wrote that participatory research is

> fundamentally a discourse about the role of knowledge and learning within the varieties of struggles in our communities for respect, fairness . . . it is about whose knowledge counts creating information for social change, recognizing indigenous and ancient knowledges and learning to be allies. (p. 174)

The results of this study were significant from a multi-level vantage point and were representative of Hall's perspective.

First, many of the incidents that the participants discussed in regard to their refugee experience in Thailand and in the United States added to the current literature in this area. The traumas that the participants and their families experienced did impact their world view. Danieli (1998) related that "what happened in one generation will affect what happens in the older or younger generation . . . " and for healing "the integration of the traumatic experience must be examined from the perspective of the totality of the trauma survivors' and family members' lives" (p. 9). This seems to ring true for Ms. Chao-Lee's family.

> The government, the CIA, brought us here without the appropriate training, not enough awareness. This has brought more trauma to us than when we were in Laos. Yes, during the war there was a lot of pain, a lot of people dying, but we didn't have to live with it. Yet, it is not the same thing.
>
> Now a lot of the folks, the older generation, they are not successful, they can't work because they never go the training. Everyday they are depressed because of that. They say, "I could do this better if I was in my country." *You know how when you have done bad, something terrible, to have the pain end like that is better than on-going all the time.*
>
> It is a reminder that a lot of our pain is because of grief. Things were not done the right way, the way that we understand, or, or even a compromise.

There was not middle road, everybody was just so far away and all of a sudden we're together. It doesn't work that way.

Boothby (1992) stated, "it has long been recognized that psychological costs may be associated with forced displacement and the process of adaptation to another socio-cultural context . . . " (p. 106). Ms. Chao-Lee clearly confirmed this.

Mr. Yaangh spoke poignantly about his experience in middle school and his struggles with peer relationships. He stated that he was "ridiculed by kids . . . shoved into a locker for no reason. The door was closed and I couldn't get out . . . kept pounding until they finally let me out." Another particular student would torment him by "messing up my hair with his hand or flicking his finger on my ear . . . the teachers did not attend to this." Mr. Yaangh's experience is echoed by Gomez (1999): "school remains an alien place for many of these [refugee] students" (p. 205). She further elaborated that "school classrooms are social, political, and cultural spaces where identity and popular memory intersect . . . the classroom is a differentiated cultural map that becomes a metaphor for other social realities in their own experiences" (Gomez, 1999, p. 204). Mr. Yaangh's experiences at school shaped his perception of the greater society and influenced his career choice. His reactions to the events led to a strong commitment to working with youth and the public school system. As a recent immigrant and adolescent entering middle school, the United States was not a warm and accepting frontier. Thus, for Ms. Lee, Mr. Yaangh, and the other participants, the process of sharing their stories was cathartic, a transformative act.

Second, the dialogues were a powerful medium for the development of generative themes in regard to cultural competency. The participants' unique experiences as recipients of social services and then providers of such services revealed insights resulting from familiarity with the two vantage points. The themes and subthemes that emerged in the course of this study made it apparent that there is a need for new approaches to the teaching of cultural competency in undergraduate social work education.

Overall, this study brings to light the importance of reflection and dialogue. It reveals that simply teaching about other cultures does not lead to cultural competency. Teaching about cultural groups may indeed perpetuate stereotypes and in turn, assumptions may be made about a particular cultural group. A more important area of focus may be teaching techniques for entering into communities such as asking questions, clarifying, and being genuine. The ability to enter a community, to demonstrate a respect and interest in that community, and to ask questions of interest were primary themes that were woven throughout all the dialogues. These seem like such simple ideas, yet perhaps in the rigor of academia, we have neglected to view the most obvious.

Many painful experiences were described as the participants recounted their experiences and reflected upon the transcripts of the initial dialogue. Each one stated on numerous occasions the same phrase, "it was/is so hard." However, the resiliency of the participants and their core desire to educate others about their culture seemed to enable them to maintain a positive and proactive outlook. Mr. Yaangh spoke well of the difficulty in discussing negative experiences due to his cultural background and the social work profession's unspoken code of respect towards other professionals. He stated that he felt the process of discussing negative events was enlightening to him: "As a social worker, we prompt families to answer negative questions. We need to experience this as a social worker to see how difficult it is [to talk of negative events]." Ms. Lee mirrored this resiliency:

> And sometimes you have to know everything so that you can survive and things like that, even avoiding being discriminated, people judges you wrongly. And don't take it so hard otherwise you would go crazy . . . you would, you would. Otherwise, you'll be dead. You wouldn't be happy at all.

The Participants' Voices

Experiences with Social Workers

The generative themes that emerged from the participants' experiences with social services suggest important changes in the undergraduate social work curriculum. The participants' experience with social workers revealed the following themes: (a) support and interest, (b) assumption versus inquiry, and (c) home versus professional roles.

Support and Interest

The participants provided examples of social workers who expressed care and insight. They described non-Iu-Mien social workers entering the Iu-Mien community through their demonstrations of genuine interest and support of their clients and colleagues. From the participant's observations, social workers who were respectful, receptive to the unfamiliar, and supportive of cultural variation developed the greatest rapport and trust from community members.

Assumption Versus Inquiry

Although the participants described social workers who exhibited cultural competency, each dialogue resonated with stories of social workers who had demonstrated their acceptance of stereotypes. Examples depicted social workers assuming that a participant and/or her or his family member lacked English language acquisition or did not provide appropriate care for her or his children or elders. When describing the incidents, the participants repeatedly stated that if the worker had inquired about the incident, asked about cultural values or for additional information, the conflicts might have been resolved without unwarranted distress.

The absence of dialogue with a Iu-Mien client reflected the type of social worker Freire (1998) warned against, those who act as instruments of oppression and do not involve "the participation of the people" (p. 14). The social workers who made assumptions exemplified extension agents, viewing their clients and colleagues from the Iu-Mien community as objects, not subjects with a voice.

Home Versus Professional Role

As each participant worked within a social service agency, a common dilemma involved the juxtaposition of their home culture and their role as a social service worker. This conflict occurred in part because of the manner they were viewed by their colleagues. The participants spoke of colleagues frequently seeing them first as a worker, rather than a member of the Iu-Mien community. Often, non-Iu-Mien workers spoke carelessly, using language that generalized, stereotyped, or offended their Iu-Mien colleagues. The non-Iu-Mien social workers were described as calling their Iu-Mien clients as "them" when talking with a Iu-Mien social service worker. This appeared to negate the worker's home culture and presented it as something foreign, strange, and, as one social worker stated, "weird." This tended to make the culture "other" while ignoring that the Iu-Mien social worker belonged to that culture.

Additionally, the participants discussed the difficulties of working with clients from their community. They expressed conflict with their role as a community member and one of authority within the social service network. This was especially difficult for those that were involved in services that followed specific laws in regard to child and elder's welfare, and domestic violence. The Iu-Mien community was described as a very strong system and one's behavior within the work setting would greatly impact relationships with family, friends, and others within the community. This was an area that each participant spoke of negotiating carefully, presenting their work role to the client and encouraging the client to share only what they would with an official in that capacity. Loyalty to the Iu-Mien community while fulfilling one's professional duties was an intricate responsibility.

Recommendations for the Teaching of Cultural Competency

The areas recommended for changes in the teaching of cultural competency in social work education include the following themes: (a) increasing knowledge of cultural differences in communication, (b) broadening experience with diversity leads to greater competence, and (c) gaining multiple perspectives of a world view.

Increasing Knowledge of Cultural Differences in Communication

There is much literature written on communication styles of varying cultural groups (Hall, 1976; Hall, & Hall, 1990; Locke, 1998; Lustig, & Koester, 1998; Lynch, & Hanson, 1998; Okun, Fried, & Okun, 1999; Stewart, & Bennett, 1991). Although the literature is rich on topic such as high and low context communication, the participants' stories resounded with examples that signified the need for greater teaching of these styles. In Ms. Chao's discussion of her presentation on Iu-Mien culture, she was asked explicit questions by a social worker in regard to domestic violence. The worker in the audience seemed to desire a statement that was precise, to the point, a "yes" or "no" answer. This is an example of a need for low-context communication. Stewart and Bennett (1991) viewed this as common among EuroAmerican people, relying "on digital, verbal messages" (p. 29) with "anticipated consequences" (p. 36). However, due to the complexity of the Iu-Mien culture in regard to "saving face" and the values and norms of the society in regard to community, a high-context communication style is common. This style of communication indicates that, "people already know that in the context of the current situation, the communicative behaviors will have a specific and particular message" (Lustig & Koester, 1998, p. 108-9).

Ms. Chao's reaction was somewhat reserved, while the social worker in the audience was direct, explicit. In a high-context culture, "the commitment between people is very strong and deep and responsibility to others takes precedence over responsibility to oneself . . . loyalties to families" (Lustig & Koester, 1999, p. 110). Stewart and Bennett (1991) highlighted this by stating,

> In all of the world outside the United States, a relationship without obligation is simply not significant . . . social act is seen as the fulfillment of an obligation or a duty and requires no verbal acknowledgement . . . |it| reveals a web of human relationships. (p. 95)

Ms. Chao, through her communication, wished to avoid conflict, a cultural value, while respecting the elders who are the most revered. The social worker's lack of knowledge of communication styles resulted in a barrier and misunderstanding of her explanation.

Ms. Chao-Lee's example of the conflict with her supervisor over apologizing to the client she interpreting for is another example of cultural differences in communication that are related to core value within a society. The supervisor initially did not understand the cultural differences. But, due to the persistence of Ms. Chao-Lee and her Western manner of addressing the conflict, she was able to resolve it and enlighten her supervisor.

In both of these examples, one could infer that ethnocentrism, believing in one's cultural superiority and exaggerating the differences in the cultures (Lustig & Koester, 1998), may have been the core of the differences. Stewart and Bennett (1991) considered ethnocentrism as "when one's own culture is considered central to all reality . . . elevated to the position of absolute truth" (p. 161). Within this context, Ms. Chao's response to the social worker in the audience and Ms. Chao-Lee's response to her Iu-Mien client may have been viewed as ambiguous due to the indirect nature (Stewart & Bennett, 1991) and thus, not seen through an Eurocentric lens as "absolute truth."

Broadening Experience with Diversity Leads to Greater Competence

All the participants related stories of social workers who demonstrated cultural competency. The common thread was that either the social worker was from a non-dominant group in the United States and/or had a transformative experience. This experience could have been simply listening without reservation to a client's story and gaining insight into the experience of oppression. Or, it may have been an altercation with a client or co-worker in regard to cultural conflict or misunderstanding that led to enlightenment.

The more a social worker was open to learning about a culture and to viewing the experience of the specific cultural group through the eyes of the client/consumer/co-worker, the greater the cultural competency. Ms. Lee stated this well:

> I have found the more they are culturally diverse, they have better understanding with that ethnic group or the culture, [the more] they can better serve them. There are ones who really wanted to learn about their culture or other ethnic culture and there are those that really don't care about it. You see that everyday at the workplace.

Mr. Yaangh reiterated these views by discussing the barrier that develops from assumptions.

> Think back to those statements about an awakening, an experience. It doesn't have to an experience with every group. It has to an experience with your own people, something that stirs them to start to think, "I am making a lot of assumptions.'" Stop and think, "I don't know." See, there lies the problem in the human service arena. We make too many assumptions. We think we know and we don't know. So, the moment we experience something that causes us to think, "okay, I don't know, I need to learn," that is when we begin to become competent.

Thus, being competent included saying, "I don't know."

Gaining Multiple Perspectives of a World View

The Iu-Mien social service workers all desired to maintain harmony while educating those about their culture. Each had numerous, sometimes daily, experiences in the United States of discrimination and prejudice. In spite of the conflicts, all desired to reframe comments and behaviors to allow themselves to work towards social change.

Ms. Chao's comments represented a sentiment common to all the participants. Prior to entering her undergraduate program, she was offended by statements regarding her culture. She felt that sometimes it was "seeming like they were doing it on purpose, being mean." However, she consciously decided to view it in a different light stating, "I just pass if off that they don't know . . . explain to them that it is okay . . . I guess the reason I just kinda stopped it [is] I don't want to deal with that." She and the other participants practiced this educational perspective daily by sharing their home, family, and traditions with non-Iu-Mien social workers.

The Participants' Recommendations

The participants in this study provided many recommendations for social work education and currently practicing social workers. Park (1993) related that "since much of the social injustice characteristic of modern society is structural in origin, participatory research acts as a catalytic intervention in social transformative process" (p. 2). Mr. Yaangh related that due to the amount of oppression, one becomes "immune to the system that you just kind of accept what is." Thus, the recommendations discussed below are indicative of the participants' process of "naming the world," formulating interventions to transform the current structure of social work education in regard to the teaching of cultural competency by naming the injustices they experienced and highlighting our rapidly changing global community.

Recommendations for Undergraduate Social Work Education

The participants' recommendations for the teaching of cultural competency focused more on gaining techniques rather than working towards a general composite of varying cultural groups. The latter is the way many cultural competency texts are formulated and courses designed. The participants spoke of teaching students the process of asking and feeling comfortable admitting "I don't know." They spoke of learning to develop questions to empower the client to share their experiences.

The general theme was humility, to be humble and not make assumptions, thereby dissolving barriers that can be erected by the need to "know it all." The participants who had received formal social work education spoke of the tendency for social workers to feel pressured to have all the answers. Many times this pressure was self-imposed due to lack of experience or knowledge. Mr. Yaangh stated that students need to have the awareness of "knowing what you don't know and humble enough to say, 'I don't know.'" He related, "it is okay to say, 'I don't know' or 'I'm not competent in this area,' or, 'I will work on it.'"

The participants also recommended immersion in a culture by working within a cultural community in an intensive, daily internship. They spoke of the need for EuroAmerican social workers to experience being a minority. Each participant felt great importance for social workers to understand a culture; they practiced this in their own lives by inviting non-Iu-Mien social workers to their cultural events and homes. They all felt that students should participate in cultural activities and be challenged to experience and interact with those from unfamiliar cultures.

Recommendations for Currently Practicing Social Workers

The participants felt that many of their recommendations for social work education were also applicable to currently practicing social workers. Each participant spoke of experiences with colleagues that caused emotional distress due to the lack of cultural competency of the co-worker. The resounding theme was for practicing social workers to be sensitive to colleagues of different cultures who are indeed social workers, but also part of a community. The participants related that they were not social workers first and, secondly, a member of a specific cultural community. They spoke of the mixture; culture is the cornerstone of one's identity, values, and behaviors.

170

The participants worked to develop a climate with co-workers for the sharing of their cultural identity. They were persistent in their openness to share. The participants recommended that social workers always ask questions when they meet someone from a cultural group who is different from theirs and that social workers be humble and open-minded. The concern was for the conscious or unconscious ethnocentrism, the Eurocentric focus that the participants commonly saw in their work settings.

Recommendations for Further Research

This study of Iu-Mien social service workers utilized participatory research methodology, Thus, the sample size was small consisting of eight individuals. The gender ratio was equal, but the age differences impacted the view of the participants. Those who came to the United States as kindergartners had a different perspective than those who came as adolescents. Additionally, some were sponsored by churches while others were sponsored by members of the Iu-Mien community.

This researcher would like to see further research on other refugee experiences from such areas as Eastern Europe, Russia, Africa, India, and South and Central Americas. Additionally, it would be important to study social workers of non-European descent who were born in the United States. Many variables would impact these studies including differences in age, country of origin, and length of time in the United States. Suggestions for further research would also be to make a greater analysis of impact of gender and ethnic background, since most social workers are EuroAmerican women.

Conclusion

Painful stories seeped throughout the research process in regard to inequity, social injustice, and discrimination in the United States. Each participant spoke of these, sometimes tagged with a positive statement, sometimes veiled in a story. Ms. Lee's account provided an overview of the accounts made by each participant:

> If you talk about discrimination though, you go through it every day. I think that everyone to some degree, they are being prejudice. Whether they are aware of it or not, they are. It does exist. What you could do so that you don't feel bad and you didn't have the intention to discriminate people, you know, judge people or be prejudice, is to get to know them and find the truth before you make assumptions.
>
> And for us, we just see it . . . people will say thing like, you were driving and people were staring at you, rolling down their window, and calling you names, telling you to go back to your country. Things like that. *Those are things we go through every single day.*

Her resiliency rang strong as she stated,

> The only thing I tell myself is not to get mad about it, the situation like that is that I think other people are not as educated as I am and I am aware of the world as diverse as I am. I am not as stupid as them. That will make me feel better. You move on . . . *you can't control what they think and say, but you can control yourself. You can improve yourself.*

Glossary

assimilation   The "process in which minority groups become absorbed or incorporated into the majority group's sociocultural system" (Bryjak & Soroka, 1997, p. 529). That is, the "implied movement from one to the other . . . " (Dirlik, 1999, p. 47), from one cultural representation to the culture of the dominant majority.

basic cultural competence   The "acceptance and respect for difference, continuing self-assessment regarding culture, careful attention to the dynamics of difference, continuous expansion of cultural knowledge and resources, and a variety of adaptations to service models in order to better meet the needs of minority populations" (Cross, 1988, pp. 1- 4).

cultural competency   "The set of knowledge and skills that a social worker must develop in order to be effective with multicultural clients . . . development of academic and professional expertise and skills in the area of working with culturally diverse clients" (Lum, 1999, p. 3). It is a developmental process, " a dynamic phenomenon; one never really 'arrives' because culture is dynamic and subject to change" (Mason, Benjamin, & Lewis, 1996, p. 177). "Cultural competency" is very common term in the field of social services. It is defined and discussed in most human service settings, having become the focal point of many continuing educational trainings and programs mandated by state and the federal government.

culturally competent practice   Effectiveness of practitioners and their agencies in considering cultural diversity issues when working with families and responding to them appropriately (Raheim, 1995).

cultural diversity   The ways people differ as a result of the patterns of norms, beliefs, and practices pertaining to their culture (Raheim, 1995).

cultural pluralism   Mutual respect for cultural differences among ethnic groups (Chau, 1989). The view of cultural pluralism provides the " . . . premise that U.S. society should not be characterized as having only one national culture, but rather it should be seen as having a national culture as well as many distinct cultural groups" (Fellin, 2000, p. 262).

ethnocentrism   The "tendency to believe that the norms and values of one's own culture are superior to those of others, and to use these norms as a standard when   evaluating all other cultures" (Bryjak & Soroka, 1997, p. 531).

Iu-Mien, Mienh, or Mien   A minority group from the highlands of Southeast Asia, practicing slash and burn agriculture, residing in small villages. They immigrated to the United States following the involvement with the CIA in the 1960s to 1975 in a "secret war" to prevent supplies to reach North Vietnamese. Most were forced to escape to Thailand, living in refugee camps until sponsored by groups or families for resettlement in the United States or other countries.

social worker   One who has received a bachelor's or master's degree in social work from a program accredited by the Council on Social Work Education. The worker is employed in a setting that provides assistance to individuals, families, groups, and communities with "their personal and social problems" (California Employment Development Department, 2000, p. 1). They may be in a supervisor position, work in state institutions such as schools, government agencies, for private agencies, or in their own clinical practice.

social service worker (or human service worker)   A high school graduate who may have some college education, and is employed in providing assistance to community members in such areas as welfare, health programs, group homes, corrections, etc., under the guidance of a supervisor (California Employment Development Department, 2000). In many cases, the social service worker needs a supervisor with a master's degree to sign off on reports due to federal and state guidelines.

References

Ada, A. F., & Beutel, C. M. (1993). *Participatory research as a dialogue for social action.* Unpublished manuscript, University of San Francisco.

Akerlund, M., & Cheung, M. (2000). Teaching beyond the deficit model: Gay and lesbian issues among African Americans, Latinos, and Asian Americans. *Journal of Social Work Education, 36* (2), 279-292.

Altpeter, M., Schopler, J. H., Maeda, J. G., & Pennell, J. (1999). Participatory research as social work practice: When is it viable? *Journal of Progressive Human Services, 10 (2),* 31-53.

Ancis, J. R. (1998). Cultural competency training at a distance: Challenges and strategies. *Journal of Counseling and Development, 76* (2), 134-43.

Anonymous. (1999). *Why me?* In K. C. Kim (Ed.), *Quietly torn (*pp. 14-15). San Francisco: Pacific News Service.

Ask.com. (2000). Welcome to 12 Clanz. Retrieved August 11, 2000: http://www.ask.com / main/askjeeves.

Atherton, S.A., & Bolland, K.A. (1997). The multiculturalism debate and social work education: A response to Dorothy Van Soest. *Journal of Social Work Education, 33* (1), 143-150.

Austin, D. M. (1997). The institutional development of social work education: The first 100 years—and beyond. *Journal of Social Work Education, 33* (3), 599-613.

Beard, T., Warrick, B., & Saefong, K. C. (Eds.). (1993). *Loz-hnoi, loz-hnoi uov . . . In the old, old days: Traditional stories of the Iu-Mien, volume 1.*Berkeley, CA: Laotian Handcraft Project, Inc.

Beard, T., Warrick, B., & Saefong, K.C. (Eds.). (1995). *Loz-hnoi, loz-hnoi uov . . . In the old, old days: Traditional stories of the Iu-Mien, volume 2.* Berkeley, CA: Laotian Handcraft Project, Inc.

Beddingfield, K.T., Hawkins, D., Ito, T. M., Lenzy, T., & Loftus, M. (1996, October 28). Twenty hot job tracks. *U. S. News & World Report, 121,* 89-96.

Bogdan, R. C., & Biklen, S. K. (1998). *Qualitative research for education: An introduction to theory and methods.* Needham Heights, MA: Allyn & Bacon.

Boothby, N. (1992). Displaced children: Psychological theory and practice from the field. *Journal of Refugee Studies, 5* (2), 106-118.

Bronstein, L., & Gibson, C. (1998). Student perceptions of content on oppression: The good news and the bad. *Journal of Teaching in Social Work, 17 (*1-20), 155-167.

Bryjak, G. J., & Soroka, M. P. (1997). *Sociology: Cultural diversity in a changing world.* Boston: Allyn and Bacon.

Burns, W. T. (1991). The changing faces of refugee education. *Cross Currents, 18* (1), 65-67.

176

California Department of Social Services. (2000). Refugee programs web site. Retrieved April 14, 2000: http://www.dss.cahwnet.gov

California Employment Development Department. (2000). Labor market information, California occupational guide number 122. Retrieved July 1, 2000: http://159.96.231/calmis search

California State Job Training Coordinating Council (SJTCC). (2000). Greater Avenues for Independence (GAIN). Retrieved April 17, 2000: http://www.ca hwnet.gov

Carrillo, D. F., & Holzhalb, C. M. (1993). Assessing social work students' attitudes related to cultural diversity: A review of selected measures. *Journal of Social Work Education, 29* (3), 263-269.

Castex, G. M. (1993). Frames of reference: The effects of ethnocentric map projections on professional practice. *Social Work, 38* (6), 685-694.

Center for Applied Linguistics. (August 1981). *The Mien: Fact sheet series #2.* Washington, DC: Office of Refugee Resettlement (DHHS).

Chao, C. C. (1999). Intergenerational relationships in Iu Mien families. Retrieved October 14, 1999: webmaster@iumien.com

Chao, K., & Saechao, K. (1999). Mien Culture. Retrieved April 11, 2000: http://www.csuchico.edu/sosw/SWK/SWK245/99-miencul.htm.

Chao, K., & Saechao, K. (2000, March) *The IU Mien culture and social worker interactions.* Paper presented at California State University, Chico, senior social work practice course, Chico, California.

Chau, K. L. (1990). A model for teaching cross-cultural practice in social work. *Journal of Social Work Education, 26* (2), 124-134.

Chau, K. L. (1992). Educating for effective group work practice in multicultural environments of the 1990s. *Journal of Multicultural Social work, 1* (4), 1-15.

Chau, K. L. (1999). Sociocultural dissonance among ethnic minority populations. *Social Casework, 70* (4), 224-230.

Chinn, S. (2000). *Mienh history and culture.* Unpublished article. Sacramento, CA.

Collins, D.E. (1977). *Paulo Freire: His life, works and thought.* New York: Paulist Press.

Collins, D. E. (2000). *Paulo Freire: Una filosofia educativa para nuestro tiempo.* Mexico: Universidad La Salle.

Comeau, M.T. (1996). *U. S. racial ideology and immigrant/refugee policy: Effects on Asian-American Identity, community formation and refugee education initiatives.* Amherst, MA: University of Massachusetts. (ERIC Document Reproduction Service No. ED 405 435)

Council on Social Work Education (CSWE). (1999). Curriculum policy statement for baccalaureate degree programs in social work education. Retrieved October 15, 1999: http://www.cswe.org/bswcps.htm

Council on Social Work Education. (2000). Membership. Retrieved November 23, 2000: http://www.cswp.org/overview.htm

Cross Cultural Health Care Program. (2000). Voices of the Mien community. Retrieved July 2, 2000: http://hermes.hslib.washington.edu/clinical/ethnomed/ voices/ mien. html

Cross, T. (1988). Services to minority populations: Cultural competence continuum. *Focal Point, 3(*1), 1-4.

Danieli, Y. (Ed.). (1998). *International Handbook of Multigenerational Legacies of Trauma.* New York: Plenum Press.

Debbink, G., & Ornelas, A. (1997). Cows for campesinos. In S. E. Smith, D. G. Willms, & N. A. Johnson (Eds.), *Nurtured by knowledge: Learning to do participatory action-research* (pp. 13-33). New York: The Apex Press.

Devore, W., & Schlesinger, E. G. (1999). *Ethnic-sensitive social work practice.* Boston: Allyn & Bacon.

Dirlik, A. (1999). Asians on the rim: Transnational capital and local community in the making of contemporary Asian America. In E. Hu-DeHart, (Ed.), *Across the Pacific: Asian Americans and globalization* (pp. 29-60). Philadelphia: Temple University Press.

Elias, J. L. (1994). *Paulo: Pedagogue of liberation.* Malabar, FL: Krieger Publishing Company.

Fadiman, A. (1997). *The spirit catches you and you fall down.* New York: Noonday Press.

Fellin, P. (2000). Revisiting multiculturalism in social work. *Journal of Social Work Education, 36* (2). 261-277.

Fong, S. M., & Saeteun, Y. K. (1989a). *Iu Mien wedding ceremony: The small wedding.* Unpublished handout.

Fong, S. M., & Saeteun, Y. K. (1989b). *Mien New Year.* Unpublished handout.

Freire, P. (1970). *Sobre la acción cultural.* Mexico: Secretariado Social Mexicano.

Freire, P. (1985). *The politics of education: Culture, power, and liberation.* New York: Bergin & Gravey Publishers, Inc.

Freire, P. (1993). Introduction. In P. Park, P., M. Brydon-Miller, B. Hall, and T. Jackson. (Eds.) *Voices of change: Participatory research in the United States and Canada.* (pp. iv-x). Westport, CT: Bergin & Garvey.

Freire, P. (1996). *Letters to Cristina.* New York: Routledge.

Freire, P. (1998). *Education for critical consciousness.* New York: Continuum Publishing Company.

Freire, P. (1999). *Pedagogy of the oppressed.* New York: Continuum Publishing Company.

Fritze, C. (2000). *Because I speak Cockney they think I'm stupid.* Retrieved January 24, 2000: http://www.community-work-training.org.uk/freire

Garcia, B., & Van Soest, D. (1997). Changing perceptions of diversity and oppression: MSW students discuss the effects of a required course. *Journal of Social Work Education, 33* (1), 131-42.

Garcia, B., & Van Soest, D. (1999). Teaching about diversity and oppression: Learning from the analysis of critical classroom events. *Journal of Teaching in Social Work, 18* (1-2), 149-167.

Giles, W. (1999) Gendered violence in war: Reflections on transnationalist and comparative frameworks in militarized conflict zones. In Doreen Indra (Ed.), *Engendering forced migration* (pp. 83-93), New York: Berghahn Books.

Gogol, S. (1996). *A Mien family.* Minneapolis, MN: Lerner Publications.

Gomez, I. (1999). A space for remembering: Home-pedagogy and exilic Latina women's identities. In Doreen Indra (Ed.), *Engendering forced migration* (pp. 200-219), New York: Berghahn Books.

Graham, M. J. (1999). The African-centered worldview. *Journal of Black Studies, 30* (1), 103-123.

Grove, P. B. (Ed.). (1976). *Webster's third new international dictionary of the English language: Unabridged.* (17th ed.). Springfield, MA: G. & C. Merriam Company.

Gutierrez, L., Fredricksen, K., & Soifer, S. (1999). Perspectives of social work faculty on diversity and societal oppression content: Results from a national survey. *Journal of Social Work Education 35* (3), 409-420.

Habarad, J. (1987a). Refugees and the structure of opportunity: Transitional adjustments to aid among U.S. resettled Lao Iu Mien, 1980-1985. In S. Morgan, & E. Colson (Eds.), *People in upheaval* (pp. 66-87). New York: Center for Migration Studies.

Habarad, J. (1987b). *The spirit and the social order: The responsiveness of Lao Iu Mien history, religion, and organization.* Unpublished doctoral dissertation, University of California, Berkeley.

Hall, B. (1993). Introduction. In P. Park, M. Brydon-Miller, B. Hall, and T. Jackson (Eds.). *Voices of change: Participatory research in the United States and Canada.* Westport, CT: Bergin & Garvey.

Hall, B. L. (2001). I wish this were a poem of practices of participatory research. In P. Reason, & H . Bradbury (Eds.) *Handbook of action research.* Thousand Oaks, CA: Sage, pp. 171-178.

Hall, E. T. (1976). *Beyond culture.* New York: Anchor Press.

Hall, E. T., & Hall, M. R. (1990). *Understanding cultural differences.* Yarmouth, ME: Intercultural Press, Inc.

Harmon, R. E. (1995). Responding to the crisis: Creation of the overseas refugee program. In D.A. Ranard & M. Pfleger (Eds.), *From the classroom to the community: A fifteen-year experiment in refugee education* (pp. 19-36). (Report No. ISBN-0-937354-55-4). Washington, DC: Center for Applied Linguistics (ERIC Document Reproduction Services No. ED 379 950).

Hemmendinger, A. (1987*). Two models for using problem-posing and cultural sharing in teaching the Hmong English as a second language and first language literacy.* Thesis, St. Francis Xavier University, Antigonish, Nova Scotia. (ERIC Document Reproduction Service No. ED342271).

Hick, S. (1997). Participatory research: An approach for structural social workers. *Journal of Progressive Human Services, 8 (2)*, pp. 63-78.

Holland, T. P., & Kilpatrick, A. C. (1993). Using narrative techniques to enhance multicultural practice. *Journal of Social Work Education, 29* (3), 302-309.

Horowitz, I. A., & Bordens, K. S. (1999). *Social psychology.* Mountain View, CA: Mayfield Publishing Company.

Houghton, T. (1989). *Iu Mien -- "The People:" An analysis of the interaction of animism, the Iu Mien and the spirit world.* Unpublished master's thesis, New College for Advanced Christian Studies, Berkeley, CA.

Hoyt, L. (1995). Enhancing the flavor: Winning partnerships between home and school. In D.A. Ranard & M. Pfleger (Eds.), *From the classroom to the community: A fifteen-year experiment in refugee education* (pp. 115-137). (Report No. ISBN-0-937354-55-4). Washington, DC: Center for Applied Linguistics (ERIC Document Reproduction Services No. ED 379 950).

Hu-DeHart, E. (1999). (Ed.). *Across the Pacific: Asian Americans and globalization.* Philadelphia: Temple University Press.

Indra, D. (1999). *Engendering forced migration.* New York: Berghahn Books.

Johnson, L. C., & Yanca, S. J. (2001). *Social work practice: A generalist approach.* Needham Heights, MA: Allyn and Bacon.

Joyappa, V., & Martin, J. D. (1996). Exploring alternative research epistemologies for adult education: Participatory research, feminist research and feminist participatory research. *Adult Education Quarterly, 47* (1), 1-14.

Kandre, P. (1967). Autonomy and integration of social systems: The Iu-Mien ("Yao" or "Man") mountain population and their neighbors. In P. Kunstadter (Ed.), *Southeast Asian tribes, minorities, and nations* (pp. 583-638). Princeton, NJ: Princeton University Press.

Kang, H., Kuehn, P., & Herrell, A. (1996). The Hmong literacy project: Parents working to preserve the past and ensure the future. *The Journal of Educational Issue of Language Minority Students, 16,* 9. Retrieved September 21, 1999: http://www.ncbe.gwu.edu.miscpubs/jeilms/vol16/jeilms1602. httm

Kieffer, C. H. (1981, April). *Doing "dialogic retrospection": Approaching empowerment through participatory research.* Paper presented at the International Meeting of the Society for Applied Anthropology, University of Edinburgh, Scotland.

Kieffer, K. M., & Leach, M. M. (1997, January). *The effects of multicultural training videos on perceived counselor competence.* Poster session presented at the annual meeting of the Southwest Educational Research Association, Texas.

Kim, K. C. (Ed.). (1999). *Quietly torn.* San Francisco: Pacific News Service.

Krajewski–Jaime, E. R., Brown, K. S., Ziefert, M., & Kaufman, E. (1996). Utilizing international clinical practice to build inter-cultural sensitivity in social work students. *Journal of Multicultural Social Work,* 4 (2), 15-29.

180

Latting, J. K. (1990). Identifying the "isms": Enabling social work students to confront their biases. *Journal of Social Work Education, 26* (1), 36-45.

Legislative Analyst's Office (LAO), State of California. (1996). Retrieved September 5, 1999: http://www.lao.ca.gov/cf96b.html

Leighninger, L. (2000). *One hundred years of teaching social workers.* Retrieved November 23, 2000: http://www.naswdc.org

Lemberger, N. (1996). *How a Spanish bilingual teacher built community in a Mien bilingual class.* Paper presented at the 1996 annual meeting of the American Educational Research Association, New York.

Lewis, P., & Lewis, E. (1984). *Peoples of the golden triangle.* New York: Thames and Hudson, Inc.

Liegel, M. (1991). Curriculum design and pre-entry training for adult Southeast Asian refugees. *Cross Currents, 18* (1), 43-52.

Ligon, F. (1995). The world of the past, the world of tomorrow: First language literacy at the Phanat Nikhom refugee camp. In D.A. Ranard & M. Pfleger (Eds.), *From the classroom to the community: A fifteen-year experiment in refugee education* (pp. 89-114).(Report No. ISBN-0-937354-55-4). Washington, DC: Center for Applied Linguistics (ERIC Document Reproduction Services No. ED 379 950).

Lindsay, J. (1996) *A rarity: Forced repatriation of the Hmong mentioned in the news.* Retrieved April 20, 2000: http://my.athenet.net/-jlindsay/HmongPC. Html

Locke, D. C. (1998). *Increasing multicultural understanding: A comprehensive model.* Thousand Oaks, CA: Sage Publications, Inc.

Long Term Care Ombudsman, (2001). *Fact sheet-Elder and dependent adult abuse: Long term care consumer guides.* Chico, CA: Passages Adult Resource Center.

Lum, D. (1999). *Culturally competent practice: A framework for growth and action.* Pacific Grove, CA: Brooks/Cole.

Lustig, M. W., & Koester, J. (1998). *Intercultural Competence: Interpersonal communication across cultures.* New York: Longman.

Lynch, E. W., & Hanson, M. J. (1998). *Developing cross-cultural competency.* Baltimore: Paul H. Brookes Publishing Company.

MacDonald, J. L. (1997.) *Transnational aspects of Iu-Mien refugee identity.* New York: Garland Publishing, Inc.

Maguire, P. (1993). Challenges, contradictions, and celebrations: Attempting participatory research as a doctoral student. In P. Park, M. Brydon-Miller, B. Hall, and T. Jackson (Eds.), *Voices of change: Participatory research in the United States and Canada* (pp. 172-185). Westport, CT: Bergin & Garvey.

Maguire, P. (1997). *Doing participatory research: A feminist approach.* Amerst, MA: Center for International Education.

Mason, J. L. (1995). *Cultural competence self-assessment questionnaire: A manual for users.* Portland, OR: Portland State University, Research and Training Center on Family Support and Children's Mental Health.

Mason, J. L., Benjamin, M. P., & Lewis, S. A. (1996). The cultural competent model: Implications for child and family mental health services. In C. A. Heflinger & C. T. Nixon (Eds.), *Families and the mental health system for children and adolescents* (pp. 165-190). Thousand Oaks, CA: Sage Publications.

McBride, M. J. (1999). *The evolution of U.S. immigration and refugee policy: public opinion, domestic politics and UNHCR.* Washington, DC: UNHCR. (Working Paper No. 3) Retrieved February 25, 2000: www. unhcr. ch/ reworld/pub/wpapers/wpno3/htm

McCoy, A. W. (1972). *The politics of heroin in Southeast Asia.* New York: Harper & Row.

McMahon, A., & Allen-Meares, P. (1992). Is social work racist? A content analysis of recent literature. *Social Work, 37* (6), 533-539.

Midgette, T. E., & Meggert, S. S. (1991). Multicultural counseling instruction: A challenge for the faculties in the 21st century. *Journal of Counseling and Development, 70* (1), 136-41.

Mingkwan, B., Kuehn P., Baker, A., Le, V., Pen, P., Ricket, J., Rose, N., & Sananikone, P. (1995). *California refugee English Language training task force: Final evaluation report.* Sacramento, CA: California State Dept. of Social Service, Office of Refugee Services. (ERIC Document Reproduction Service No. ED 394 362).

Moore-Howard, P. (1989). *The Iu-Mien tradition and change.* Sacramento, CA: Sacramento City Unified School District.

Morgan, A. (1995). Balancing the ideal and the pragmatic: Reflections on the overseas refugee program. In D.A. Ranard & M. Pfleger (Eds.), *From the classroom to the community: A fifteen-year experiment in refugee education* (pp. 1-18). (Report No. ISBN-0-937354-55-4). Washington, DC: Center for Applied Linguistics. (ERIC Document Reproduction Services No. ED 379 950).

Morris, J. K. (1993). Interacting oppressions: Teaching social work content on women of color. *Journal of Social Work Education, 29* (1), 99-111.

Moua, S. (2000). *Living in Thailand.* Retrieved April 23, 2000: http://ww2.saturn.stpaul.k12.mn.us/hmong/studentshowcase/studentshowc ase/storybook/

Mueke, M. (1983). Caring for southeast Asian refugees in the USA. *American Journal of Public Health, 73* (4), 431-438.

Nagda, B.A., Spearmon, M.L., Holley, L. C., Harding, S., Balassone, M. S., Moise-Swanson, D., & de Mello, S. (1999). Intergroup dialogues: An innovative approach to teaching about diversity and justice in social work programs. *Journal of Social Work Education, 35* (3), 433-50.

Nakasako, S. (Producer and Director). (1998). *Kelly loves Tony* [Film]. (Available from National Asian American Telecommunications Association (NAATA), 346 Ninth Street, Second Floor, San Francisco, CA 94103)

National Association of Social Workers. (1997). *Code of ethics.* Washington, DC: Author.

National Association of Social Workers. (2000). Overview. Retrieved November 23, 2000: http://www.naswdc.org

Okun, B. F., Fried, J., & Okun, M. L. (1999). *Understanding diversity: A learning-as-practice primer.* Pacific Grove, CA: Brooks/Cole Publishing Company.

Park, P. (1989). *What is participatory research? A theoretical and methodological perspective.* Manuscript submitted for publication. Northampton, MA: Center for Community Education & Action, Inc.

Park, P. (1993). What is participatory research? A theoretical and methodological perspective. In P. Park, M. Brydon-Miller, B. Hall, and T. Jackson (Eds.), *Voices of change: Participatory research in the United States and Canada* (pp. 12-21). Westport, CT: Bergin & Garvey.

Patton, M. Q. (1990). *Qualitative evaluation and research methods.* Newbury Park, CA: Sage Publications, Inc.

Petras, E., & Porpora D. V. (1993). Participatory Research: Three models and an analysis. *The American Sociologist, 24*, (1), 107-126.

Phillips, J. M. (1995). Beyond the classroom: Meeting the needs of young adult Amerasians. In D.A. Ranard & M. Pfleger (Eds.), *From the classroom to the community: A fifteen-year experiment in refugee education.* (pp. 69-88) (Report No. ISBN-0-937354-55-4). Washington, DC: Center for Applied Linguistics (ERIC Document Reproduction Services No. ED 379 950)

Pierce, D., & Taitano, K. (1999). Lesbian and gay lives: Simulating oppression and social change. *Journal of Teaching in Social Work, 19* (1/2), 109-122.

Pinderhughes, E. (1997). Developing diversity competence in child welfare and permanency planning. *Journal of Multicultural Social Work, 5* (1/2), 19-38.

Pon, E. M. (1984). *The Hmong and Mien: Beyond esl training programs.* Paper presented at the National Association for Interdisciplinary Ethnic Studies, Inc., Kansas City, MO.

Poole, D. L. (1998). Politically correct or culturally competent? *Health and Social Work, 23* (3), 163-67.

Potocky, M. (1997). Multicultural social work in the United States: A review and critique. *International Social Work, 40* (3), 315-326.

Raheim, S. (1995). Culturally competent practice in family centered services. In B. K. Williams (Ed.), *Family centered services: A handbook for practitioners* (pp. 24-35). Iowa City, IA: National Resource Center on Family Based Services.

Ranard, D. A., & Pfleger, M. (1993). Language and literacy education for southeast Asian refugees. *National Clearinghouse on Literacy Education, EDO-LE-93-06.__* (pp. 4). Retrieved September 24, 1999: http://www.cal.org ncle/DIGESTS/ SEASIAN.HTML

Ranard, D.A., & Pfleger, M. (Eds.). (1995). Redefining survival: Practices, trends, and the issues in the overseas refugee program. In D.A. Ranard & M. Pfleger (Eds.), *From the classroom to the community: A fifteen-year experiment in refugee education* (pp. 37-68). (Report No. ISBN-0-937354-55-4). Washington, DC: Center for Applied Linguistics (ERIC Document Reproduction Services No. ED 379 950)

Randall-David, E. (1994). *Culturally competent HIV counseling and education.* McAllen, VA: Maternal and Child Health Clearinghouse.

Reason, P. (1994). *Three approaches to participative inquiry.* In B. Norman, K. Design, & F. S. Lincoln, (Eds.). *Handbook of qualitative research* (pp. 324-339). Beverly Hills, CA: Sage Publications, Inc.

Rittner, B., Nakanishi, M., Nackerud, L., & Hammons, K. (1999). How MSW graduates apply what they learned about diversity to their work with small groups. *Journal of Social Work Education, 35* (3), 421-431.

Rodriguez, J. C. (1993). Reconstruction of academic credentials for southeast Asian refugee teachers: A comprehensive IHE approach to access and excellence. In L. M. Malave (Ed.), *Proceedings of the national association for bilingual education conferences, (Tucson, AZ, 1990; Washington, DC, 1991),* (pp. 191-196). Washington, DC: National Association for Bilingual Education.

Saechao, F. L. (1999a). America. In K. C. Kim (Ed.), *Quietly Torn* (pp. 50-51). San Francisco: Pacific News Press.

Saechao, F. L. (1999b). No freedom to choose arranged marriages. In K. C. Kim (Ed.), *Quietly torn (*p. 18). San Francisco: Pacific News Service.

Saechao, L. C. (1993). The trials of the orphan brothers. In T. Beard, B. Warrick, & K. C. Saefong (Eds.), *Loz-hnoi, loz-hnoi uov . . . In the old, old days: Traditional stories of the Iu-Mien, volume 1* (pp. 56-61). Berkeley, CA: Laotian Handcraft Project, Inc.

Saechao, L. C. (1999). Animism-the ancestors are always there for us. In K. C. Kim (Ed.), *Quietly torn (*p. 26). San Francisco: Pacific News Service.

Saechao, M. L. (1999). Gender roles and rules. In K. C. Kim (Ed.), *Quietly torn* (pp. 8-9). San Francisco: Pacific News Service.

Saechao, Y. W. (1999a). Chio Choy. In K. C. Kim (Ed.), *Quietly torn (*p. 16). San Francisco: Pacific News Service.

Saechao, Y. W. (1999b). My community, my church. In K. C. Kim (Ed.), *Quietly torn (*p. 29). San Francisco: Pacific News Service.

Saephan, C. M. (1995). The Yiem-Fiu Mien and the orphan. In T. Beard, B. Warrick, & K. C. Saefong, (Eds.). *Loz-hnoi, loz-hnoi uov . . . In the old, old days: Traditional stories of the Iu-Mien, volume 2* (pp. 27-32). Berkeley, CA: Laotian Handcraft Project, Inc.

184

Saephan, M. H. (1999). Being a Christian. In K. C. Kim (Ed.), *Quietly torn* (p. 28). San Francisco: Pacific News Service.

Saetern, C. C. (2000). The Iu-Mien of Laos. Retrieved July 2, 2000 from the http://www.mekongexpress.com/laos/articles/dc_0995_thelumien.html

Saetern, M. K. (1998). *Iu Mien in America: Who we are.* Oakland, CA: Graphic House Press.

Said, E. W. (1978). *Orientalism.* New York: Random House.

Schultz, S. L. (1982). How Southeast-Asian refugees in California adapt to unfamiliar health care practices. *Health and Social Work, 7,* 148-155.

Simich-Dudgeon, C. (1989). English literacy development: Approaches and strategies that work with limited English proficient children and adults. *NCBE New Focus: Occasional Papers in Bilingual Education, 12* (p. 11). Retrieved September 24, 1999: http://ncbe.gwu.edu/ncbepubs/classics/Focus/12eld.htm/

Singleton, S. M. (1994). Faculty personal comfort and the teaching of content on racial oppression. *Journal of Multicultural Social Work, 3* (1), 5-16.

Smith, M.P., & Tarallo, B. (1993*). California's changing faces: New immigrant survival strategies and state policy.* Berkeley, CA: University of California Press.

Smith, S., Willms, D. G., & Johnson, N. A., (1997). (Eds.). *Nurtured by knowledge: Learning to do participatory action-research.* New York: The Apex Press.

Stewart, E. C., & Bennett, M. J. (1991). *American cultural patterns.* Yarmouth, ME: Intercultural Press, Inc.

Strouse, J. (1989). *Educational policy and the Hmong.* Paper presented at the American Educational Research Association, San Francisco.

Takaki, R. (1998). *Strangers from a different shore.* New York: Back Bay Books.

Tasker, M. (1999). "You like Tupac, Mary?" *Families in Society: The Journal of Contemporary Human Services, 80* (3). Retrieved October 22, 1999: http://web7.infotrac.galegroup.com

Smith, T. B. (Ed.) (2004). *Practicing multiculturalism.* Boston: Pearson Education, Inc.

Taylor, P. V. (1993). *The texts of Paulo Freire.* Philadelphia: Open University Press.

Taylor-Brown, S., Garcia, A., & Kingson, E. (2001). Cultural competence versus cultural chauvinism: Implications for social work. *Health and Social Work, 26* (3), 185-187.

Tollefson, J. S. (1991). Meeting the long-term educational needs of resettled refugees: An integrated approach. *Cross Currents, 18* (1), 91-98.

Trattner, W. I. (1974). *From poor law to welfare state.* New York: The Free Press.

United States Bureau of Labor Statistics. (2004). Retrieved May 12, 2004: http://www.bls.gov/oco/pcps060.htm#outlook.

United States Census Bureau, *The foreign born population in the United States.* Retrieved August 12, 2001: http:://www.csnsus.gov/prod/2000pubs/p. 20-534pdf

United States Census Bureau, *2000 supplementary survey.* Retrieved August 12, 2001:http://www.census.gov/c2ss/www/productr/profiles/2000/narrative

United States Department of State. (2000). *Questions and answers about the United States refugee resettlement program.*. Retrieved April 22, 2000: http://www.cal.org /rsc/qa/qaeng.htm

University of California, Irvine. Southeast Asian archive. *Resettlement.* Retrieved April 14, 2000: http://www.lib.uci.edu/new/seaexhibit

Van Soest, D. (1995). Multiculturalism and social work education: The non-debate about competing perspectives. *Journal of Social Work Education, 31* (1), 55-66.

Van Soest, D. (2000). Using an interactive website to educate about cultural diversity and societal oppression. *Journal of Social Work Education, 36* (3). 463-480.

Van Soest, D. J. (1994). Social work education for multicultural practice and social justice advocacy: A field study of how students experience the learning process. *Journal of Multicultural Social work, 3* (1), 17-28.

Van Voorhis, R.M. (1998). Culturally relevant practice: A framework for teaching the psychosocial dynamics of oppression. *Journal of Social Work Education, 3* (1), 121-123.

Vuong, V., & Huynh, J. D. (1992). *Southeast Asians in the United States: A strategy for accelerated and balanced integration.* In F. G. Rivera & J. L. Erlic (Eds.), *Community organizing in a diverse society* (pp. 201-222). Boston: Allyn and Bacon.

Wallerstein, N. (1983). Problem-posing can help students learn: From refugee camps to resettlement country classrooms. *TESOL Newsletter, 10,* 28-30.

Waters, T. (1990). Adaptation and migration among the Mien people of Southeast Asia. *Ethnic Groups, 8,* 127-141.

Waters, T. (1999). *Crime and immigrant youth.* Thousand Oaks, CA: Sage Publications, Inc.

Weaver, H. N. (1999). Indigenous people and the social work profession: Defining culturally competent services. *Social Work, 44* (3), 217-226.

Weinstein-Shr, G. (1994). From mountaintops to city streets: Literacy in Philadelphia's Hmong community. In B. J. Moss (Ed.), *Literacy across communities* (pp. 49-83). Cresskill, NY: Hampton Press, Inc.

Wolfson, G. (1992). *Towards cross cultural sensitivity in the human services.* Abbotsford, B.C.: University College of the Fraser Valley Press.

Yaangh, C. (2001). *A study of successful Iu-Mien high school graduates.* Unpublished master's thesis, California State University, Sacramento, CA.

Yuen, F. K. O., & Pardeck, J. T. (1998). Impact of human diversity education on social work students. *International Journal of Adolescence and Youth, 7* (3), 249-261.

Name Index

A
Ada, A. F., 98,99,106
Akerlund, M., 82
Allen-Meares, P., 7,81,95
Altpeter, M., 100
Ancis, J. R., 91
Atherton, S.A., 90
Austin, D. M., 79

B
Baker, A., 33
Balassone, M. S., 7,93
Beard, T., 68
Beddingfield, K.T., 4
Bennett, M. J., 165,166
Beutel, C. M., 98,99,106
Biklen, S. K., 97
Bogdan, R. C., 97
Bolland, K.A., 90
Boothby, N., 161
Borden, K. S., 148
Bronstein, L., 85,86
Brown, K. S., 91,94
Bryjak, G. J., 10,173
Burns, W. T., 24,27

C
Castex, G. M., 7,79
Chao, 7,8,30,61,39,41,42,45,46, 48,
   50,57,70, 110,111-113,124,126,
   128-131,133,137,137-143,145,
   146,149,151-157,160,161,165,
   166,168
Chao, C. C., 176
Chao, K., xviii,107,110
Chao-Lee, M. M., xviii,3,8,110-113,
   124,126,130,137-140,142,143,
   149,151-154,156,160,161,166
Chau, K. L., 39,80,90,91
Cheung, M., 82
Chinn, S., xviii,5,18,56,67,110,113,
   114,126,133,136,144,146,155
Chinn, Sunny, 110
Collins, D.E., xvii,73,75,99
Comeau, M.T., 24-26,28

Cross, T., 4,37,49,173

D
Danieli, Y., 160
de Mello, S., 7,93
Debbink, G., 99
Devore, W., 1
Dirlik, A., 173

E
Elias, J. L., 99

F
Fadiman, A., 25,64,109,133
Fellin, P., 11,173
Fong, S. M., 42,43,57
Fredricksen, K., 89
Freire, P., xvii,9,10,73-77,98,99,101,
   123,163
Fried, J., 165
Fritze, C., 75

G
Garcia, 80,81,84,85,91
Gibson, C., 85,86
Giles, W., 18
Gogol, S., 5,43,61,69
Gomez, I., 161
Graham, M. J., 7,10,79,80
Gutierrez, L., 89

H
Habarad, J., 8,27,30,51,55,57,59,62,
   63,71
Hall, 98,123,160
Hanson, M. J., 165
Harding, S., 7,93
Harmon, R. E., 18-20,26,69
Hawkins, D., 4
Hemmendinger, A., 34
Herrell, A., 31
Hick, S., 101
Hmong, xiii,8,15,22,23,29,30,32-34,36,
   64,66,68,69,112,119,120,128
Holland, T. P., 92

Subject Index

A

adult abuse, defined, 135
Adult Protective Services (APS), 116, 132,135
Aid to families with dependent children (AFDC), 25,27
Armee clandestine, 68
assimilation (defined), 9-11,25,37,73,77, 78,81

B

Bataan, 17,19,23

C

California State Job Training Coordinating Council (SJTCC), 26
California Work Opportunity and Responsibility to Kids (CalWorks), 26,111,116
Cambodia(n), 15,23,27,69
Center for Applied Linguistics, 19,23, 37,66
child abuse, xv,134
Child protective services (CPS), 116, 132-134,146
China, 37,38,53,68,114
Chinese, 12,17,30,32,37,39,41,43,44, 53,54,66,67,70,107
CIA, 8,57,64,67-70,160
    Secret war, 7,8,69,70,173
Communist, 17,64,69,112
Council on Social Work Education (CSWE), 6,10,13,78,79,89,95
Communication, xiii,3,12,18,22,28,31-33,39,40,48,54,61,63-67,69
    Audio letters, 107,111
    Circular letters, 64-66
    Cross cultural, 34
    High context/ Low context, xi, xiii-xiv, 31, 165
    Court system, 117
Cross Cultural Health Care Program, 37, 49
cultural competency (defined), xi,xii, xiv,xvi,2,4-7,9-13,15,73,77,78,80,
87,89,91,95,97,104,105,112,113, 120,132,135,138,139,143,148,150-152,154,156,159,160-163,165-169
    assumptions, 99,124,127-129, 132,151,156,157,162,164, 167,169,171
        clients, xiii,xv,1,2,6,8, 10,74-164
        colleagues, xvii,2,12,13, 84,133,137,138, 143,146,147,163, 164,169
    practitioners, 6
    basic (defined),8,18,20,25,32, 36,65,77, 87,124,151
    crime , 60
        domestic violence, 49
        youth, 32
    cultural immersion, 6
    cultural values, xiii,49,60,106, 127,142,143
    education, 66
        curriculum, xiii,1,5-7,9,10, 12,13,19,23,24,33,79, 83,89,163
        defined, 10
        stereotypes, 7,79,82,90,92, 93,95,127,162,163
        textbooks, 23
    experience, xii,xiii,23
    ethical standard, 5,77
    mentor, xvii,149
    home culture, 2.164
    inquiry, 124,151,163,169
    internship, 151,169
    language, 20
    outreach, 113,120,151,155
    practice, 1-3-6,9,13,54,65,73,77, 80,81,87-89,91,92,94,95,99, 100,102,121,133,155,168, 169
    respect, xi,xii,xiii,2,16,40,48,49, 57,70,84,91,95,104,109, 117,124,131,136,143,149, 154,160,162

192

MELLEN STUDIES IN SOCIAL WORK